Kristen Suzanne's
EASY Raw Vegan Transition Recipes

OTHER BOOKS BY KRISTEN SUZANNE

Kristen's Raw: The EASY Way to Get Started & Succeed at the Raw Food Vegan Diet & Lifestyle

Kristen Suzanne's EASY Raw Vegan Entrees

Kristen Suzanne's EASY Raw Vegan Desserts

Kristen Suzanne's EASY Raw Vegan Soups

Kristen Suzanne's EASY Raw Vegan Salads & Dressings

Kristen Suzanne's EASY Raw Vegan Smoothies, Juices, Elixirs & Drinks (includes wine drinks!)

Kristen Suzanne's EASY Raw Vegan Sides & Snacks

Kristen Suzanne's EASY Raw Vegan Holidays

Kristen Suzanne's EASY Raw Vegan Dehydrating

Kristen Suzanne's Ultimate Raw Vegan Hemp Recipes

Kristen Suzanne's Ultimate Raw Vegan Chocolate Recipes

For details, Raw Food resources, and Kristen's free Raw Food newsletter, please visit:

KristensRaw.com

Kristen Suzanne's

EASY Raw Vegan Transition Recipes

• •

Fast, Easy, Raw and Cooked Vegan Recipes
to Help You and Your Family Start Migrating
Toward the World's Healthiest Diet

by Kristen Suzanne

*Green
Butterfly
Press*

Scottsdale, Arizona

Green Butterfly Press
19550 N. Gray Hawk Drive, Suite 1042
Scottsdale, AZ 85255 USA

Library of Congress Control Number: 2010934278
Library of Congress Subject Heading:
1. Cookery (Natural foods) 2. Raw foods

ISBN: 978-0-9823722-1-0

1.0

Contents

• • • • • • • • •

3: Sneaky Transition Recipes (They'll Never Know!)   71

4: Raw Recipes to Make You Dance! 89

Recipe List

PHOTOS OF SELECT RECIPES FROM THIS BOOK

See KristensRaw.com/photos

To keep the price of this book as low as possible, we've put color photos online. (Note: ebook versions of my books have color photos included.)

For enticing color photographs of the following recipes found in this book, visit *KristensRaw.com/photos*:

- Cheezy Corkscrew Macaroni
- Fiesta Tostadas
- Ginger Spice Carrot Cake
- "Give Me More!" Stuffed Bell Peppers
- Hearty Buckwheat Biscuits
- Kristen Suzanne's Italian Lasagna #2
- Mushroom Vegetable Harvest Soup
- Paradise Mango & Pâté Wrap
- Plant Power Burgers
- Protein Pesto Pasta
- Rustic Country Breakfast
- Savory Garden Vegetables with Buckwheat Noodles
- Sweet Coconut Oat Bars
- Vegan Pepperoni Pizza
- Vibrant Green Chia Pudding

1
. . .

Why Transition to Raw & Vegan Foods?

This world belongs to the energetic.

RALPH WALDO EMERSON

THE ULTIMATE VERSION OF "EATING WELL"

There is a food ladder in our culture, and everybody is somewhere on that ladder. One of the most interesting aspects of the ladder is that, no matter where you are on the ladder, the next step up seems extreme because it's usually unfamiliar. Crappy eaters think omnivores who eat "health-food" are extreme because they don't add lots of butter and salt to their food. But omnivores think vegetarians are extreme. Vegetarians think vegans are extreme. And vegans think Raw fooders are extreme. In reality, none of these are extreme. There is just "what you are used to." Once you're accustomed to any diet, it becomes your normal way of life, and it is only extreme to somebody else. This sequence of steps form a conceptual "ladder" that is very important because it will help you remember that the process of transitioning from where you are today, to eating the healthiest way possible, is not a giant, difficult, improbable leap. Rather, it's a series of smaller, relatively easy baby steps as you work your way up the ladder.

Bottoming out on the lowest rung of the ladder is what many people call the Standard American Diet, or "S.A.D." And yes, it literally is sad, because it's so filled with awful, processed, high-fat, high-calorie, low-nutrient foods that it kills millions of people a year via heart disease, diabetes, high blood pressure, obesity, and other common ailments that are almost entirely preventable.

The next rung up on the ladder refers to many people who think they are eating "healthy." Anybody who routinely eats, for instance, a dinner of chicken, brown rice, and steamed broccoli (without butter and salt) falls into this category. They avoid over-indulging in sweets and fried foods; perhaps trying to eat chicken or fish instead of hamburger; or egg whites instead of whole eggs. They try to eat whole grain breads instead of white bread, and maybe a little more fruits and vegetables than their S.A.D friends, co-workers, and family members. S.A.D. people often find this avoidance of French fries, burgers, and fatty desserts as extreme, or impractical. But it's all relative; to the "healthy" eater, these foods are just normal, and the S.A.D. junk food diet is very unappealing, or even a little disgusting. And this so-called "healthy" diet is certainly healthier than the S.A.D. diet, but there's a problem: It's still not healthy.

Most people do not realize, for instance, that chicken has just as much cholesterol as beef. But for their efforts at eating better than S.A.D. eaters, the "healthy" eaters' doctors tell them they're doing great, especially if their blood cholesterol is below 200. In reality, these people are merely healthier than the *average*, in a culture where "average" is extremely unhealthy, overweight, diseased, and likely to die an early death of heart disease or some other diet- and lifestyle-related disease. These so-called "healthy" eaters are like C students who feel really smart because they're in a remedial class full of F students. Meanwhile, there exists a whole higher echelon of health that is such a small percentage of the population that most doctors don't even know that much about it. These are the vegans.

A "vegan" diet is one in which a person consumes no animal products. That means no animal flesh (meat, fish, chicken, etc.), no eggs, and no dairy (milk, cheese, ice cream, yogurt, etc.). Strict vegans do not even eat honey, because it comes from bees. Being vegan also means not eating foods that have "hidden" animal-based ingredients, such as the milk in most non-dark chocolate, or gelatin in marshmallows.

For vegans, it is not at all unusual to have a blood cholesterol level below 150! Ignore the S.A.D.-skewed average, this 150 is the level that *all* people should be aiming for!... at least, the ones who like staying alive. Cholesterol does not exist in any plant-based food; it's only found in animal-based foods. Our bodies manufacture all we need, and we have a hard time breaking down cholesterol that we eat, which is why it ends up gunking up our arteries and killing us prematurely. In fact, the ideal amount of dietary cholesterol is 0, as in "none." The only way to achieve this is to eat no animal products.

Aside from having far lower than average cholesterol, vegans generally enjoy lower risks of many diseases. That said, not all vegan diets are healthy. After all, Oreos and Twizzlers are vegan. The term "junk food vegan" exists for a reason. It applies to vegans who consume disproportionate amounts of sugar, processed flour, and fats, as opposed to fruits, vegetables, whole grains, and avoiding overly processed foods that are devoid of nutritional value.

Healthy vegans, on the other hand, eat very well: Lots of vegetables, fruits, whole grains, and plant-based sources of protein such as soy, tempeh, seitan, beans, lentils, quinoa, millet, and others. (They also make sure they get plenty of vitamin B12, usually via a daily multivitamin.) I firmly believe that, from a health and longevity perspective, this is the minimum acceptable level of eating on the ladder. Anything less is a prescription for health problems either now or later on down the road.

If you are currently eating a lot of animal-based foods, I would encourage you to phase them out. Some people do this all at once, *cold turkey*... as it were. Others do it over a period of time, as they take incremental steps and gradually learn how to find or prepare plant-based alternatives.

BUT WAIT... THERE'S SOMETHING EVEN HEALTHIER!

Going "Raw" takes vegan to a whole other level... in fact, once you try Raw, vegan won't seem extreme at all. Cooked vegan food might even seem decadent, until your palette adjusts to the delicious freshness of a Raw (or "High Raw") diet. (I often capitalize "Raw" when referring to the Raw cuisine or lifestyle, as opposed to a specific ingredient that hasn't been cooked.)

As a cuisine, most Raw fooders define "Raw" as any plant-based food that has not been heated above 118 degrees F. (Technically, meat, eggs, and dairy can be raw/unpasteurized, but very few people advise eating these raw for risk of contracting food-borne illness. When you hear about the "Raw food" diet or lifestyle, it almost exclusively refers to raw vegan foods.)

Some Raw fooders eat 100% of their food raw, but I find that more often Raw fooders are known as "High Raw," the definition of which varies from one person to another, but generally means that 75-85% of their food is uncooked. You can think of it as meaning simply, "mostly Raw."

WHAT THIS MEANS FOR YOU

The great thing about the Raw food lifestyle is that it's not all-or-none. You can start with a little or a lot! You can work your way toward your goal slowly, quickly, or anywhere in-between. You can even take breaks, or switch things up now and then, or indulge some cooked vegan goodies, say, while traveling, or during the holidays or colder weather, only to clean up your diet come New Years or when spring time hits. Whatever works for you is absolutely fine!

This book is called "Transitions" for a reason! The main idea is that, wherever you are on the food ladder today, you can immediately start transitioning toward eating more Raw and vegan foods, without necessarily feeling like you're making some huge religious irreversible conversion. Raw food isn't like that at all! (Well, for most people.) Raw food is fun! It's easy to do (I mean, think about it... you're basically "not cooking"... how hard can it be?)

Most of all, Raw food is extremely rewarding as you start feeling better, having more energy, and getting lean-n-healthy. *Have fun with it!*

NEW TO RAW?

If you are new to Raw food, be sure to see Appendix A for lots of helpful tips on the vegan and Raw lifestyle. (Even if you are not new to Raw, you might find some helpful information so be sure to take a look.)

Also, be sure to check out the resources listed in Appendix B.

TRANSITION RECIPES... AND WHAT MAKES THEM SO SPECIAL

I decided to write a book with Raw Vegan Transition Recipes because I hear from so many people who are excited about the idea of Raw food, but they get intimidated by the idea of fundamentally changing their lifestyle, or they just want to take things nice n' easy. For those people I say, *no problem!* This book is for people who just want to test the waters, or maybe they know they'd like to transition, but they want to do so more gradually.

As a consultant, I am asked two questions: 1) "How can I get into Raw gradually?" and 2) "My family is not going to be happy about eating all Raw... What can I do?" For these people, these recipes are perfect, a great way to get more Raw into your life without committing to "going Raw" 100%, or when your family is resistant to the idea of giving up their unhealthy comfort foods for super healthy meals.

These recipes are a great way to sneak more raw vegan foods into both your and your family's lives, and in most, if not all, cases... they won't even realize it because the recipes contain elements of both the familiar and the new, in one integrated dish. If it's just about helping you transition to a Raw vegan diet for yourself, then you will love the way you can gently walk into the Raw lifestyle with these recipes.

In my own journey with pregnancy, there were times that I wanted more protein in my diet and these recipes were instrumental in helping me accomplish that. This is also a great book for people who like living a High Raw lifestyle. I, myself, go back and forth between All-Raw and High Raw fairly often. For instance, cooked foods are nice for keeping warmer during the winter. These recipes are perfect for those times I want a little cooked food without overdoing it.

The great thing about these recipes is that they have a wonderful combination of textures and flavors. About 30–50% of each "partly Raw" dish has an "om nom nom," mushy factor that is very satisfying. Yet, when you look at the recipes' raw ingredients, you see that you're also getting some fierce mega nutrition. There's more to life than mush. For many people, Raw gives a texture that is very refreshing. They come to love it as much as they used to love comfort food texture. Raw food often has plenty of crunch from the fresh produce's abundant water and fiber. If you combine that refreshing texture with some yummy soft cooked vegan foods, you have a winning and fun combination that can make your taste buds, as well as your soul, happy, and bring you closer to Raw without even knowing it's happening.

I have also included many All-Raw recipes in this book. I created these "must make" recipes so that when you're ready for the next step toward trying All-Raw recipes, you'll already have the recipes in your hand, meaning the only barrier between you and trying true Raw is a trip to the grocery store!

THREE GROUPS OF RECIPES

This book's recipes are divided into three sections:

Chapter 2: Partly Raw Recipes to Knock Your Socks Off!

These are some of the delicious "partly Raw" (all vegan) transition recipes described above, designed to help you transition from cooked to Raw vegan foods by combining some cooked with some Raw foods.

Raw foods have a unique flavor profile and often have textures that are very different from cooked foods. Again, mashed potatoes and other comfort foods might sound more appealing, but they are much less healthy than eating Raw.

There are two tricks for overcoming this. The first is to use recipes that utilize Raw foods in ways that taste really, *really* good and sometimes employing creative textures that are similar to comfort foods. The second is to gradually become accustomed to eating Raw foods, and letting your taste buds and palate adapt. Once you start eating more Raw, if you're making recipes you love, then you really will start to change. Eventually, those old "comfort" foods won't be nearly as appealing as they used to be. As you start learning to appreciate and truly experience living, healthy, vibrant foods, those old mushy dishes will literally start to taste "dead" and flavorless, or so heavily processed that they just lose their appeal.

Chapter 3: Sneaky Transition Recipes

These are similar to the transition recipes in Chapter 2, except that they have been developed specifically for helping you introduce more Raw foods into your family's diet… without them realizing it!

We'll accomplish this by introducing partly-Raw foods that people are already familiar with. For instance, guacamole is already Raw, meaning no guac-lover in your family is going to say, "Hey, why isn't this guacamole cooked?" From their point of view, these recipes will just seem like variants of something ordinary, rather than a whole new cuisine. But we're going to be sneaking in elements that are foundational to the Raw cuisine. As their taste buds and palates adapt, they'll become more receptive to dishes that have increasingly more Raw and fewer cooked components. Now you can see why we call them *sneaky!*

Chapter 4: 100% Raw Recipes!

My goal is to give you a number of transition recipes that help you transition your palate and prepare it for 100% Raw recipes. It wouldn't do for me to help you refurbish your palate and just leave you hanging there, so I've included a chapter of delicious 100% All-Raw recipes to get you started. They're hand-picked to be easy and addictively good, meaning once you try them, you'll be hooked and wanting more.

To help make your journey and transition as easy as possible, throughout the book, I have suggested variations in many of the recipes. These variations give you options that allow you to be more flexible, such as if a recipe calls for an ingredient you or a family member doesn't like, or is out of season, or if you've already got something else on-hand in your kitchen and don't want to make an extra trip to the store.

For example, if a dish includes kale, you can substitute the kale with swiss chard, collard greens, bok choy, etc. If a recipe calls for cooked lentils, then you can use black beans, millet, quinoa, or buckwheat for the warm, cooked ingredient. You should also feel free to mix up the various vegetables and fruits. Therefore, you have loads of variations on many of these recipes, making for all kinds of new recipes, which creates excitement, motivation, and a whole new creative dimension. Just be sure to write down what you are doing if you're not following the ingredients I've listed, so you don't forget what you've made, or how you made it!

A SPECIAL CHALLENGE: CHEESE

And now a special note on a strategy to help with the transition to vegan if you aren't one already...

If you don't like cheese, then the following doesn't apply to you. For everyone else, when people first try going vegan, many of them fail due to one food in particular: Cheese! Even if they don't realize it, almost everybody loves cheese... just imagine your favorite pizza without it! (If you're lactose intolerant, you have probably eaten a fair amount of cheeseless pizza.)

Cheese has a special place among foods, especially as an ingredient in cooked dishes, due to its gooey texture when melted. People might not realize they have a particular love of cheese, that is, until it's taken away. Suddenly, a lot of foods just don't seem "right" without it. If a craving hits during a moment of weakness, it's easy to see how somebody might slip back to his or her old ways.

For years, vegan cheese substitutes attempted to fill this void, but with limited success. Soy-based vegan cheeses never really melted right. Those that melted well were not vegan, because they included casein, a milk protein.

For years and years, it looked as though vegans were just out of luck on the cheese front. And then something wonderful happened that changed everything...

Daiya™ to the Rescue!

In 2009, a Canadian company called Daiya introduced what many vegans believe is the world's best vegan cheese substitute. Available in two flavors (a yellow cheddar and a white Italian blend) Daiya burst onto the scene initially in a few restaurants around the country. It has since swept the vegan world and now is available direct to consumers in many health food stores, including Whole Foods Market.

Daiya's cheeses won VegNews Magazine's 2009 Product of the Year award. This is an amazing vegan cheese that is reputed as "the cheese to keep vegans vegan." Therefore, for many, it has been truly life-changing, not just as a great cheese substitute, but because it makes the whole diet workable for many who had formerly had problems sticking to it every time they walked past a pizzeria with pizza-by-the-slice sitting in the window.

Daiya cheese is non-dairy, non-soy, non-gluten, non-rice, non-corn, non-nut, non-preservatives. (It's actually made out of tapioca root, but you'd never know.) It's absolutely amazing, both in flavor and texture. Best of all, it melts like real cheese!

Keep in mind, Daiya is not consumed raw, so this breakthrough is for cooked-food vegans, not Raw fooders... unless of course, you're not 100% Raw, which is the whole point of this book!

Ultimately, the goal should be to have *Raw* cheese as the primary cheese in your life, not Daiya. Raw cheese is delicious. It's made out of nuts and flavored to resemble cheese. However, as a nice transition cheese away from animal-based cheese, as well as having as a cooked treat from time-to-time even when you're mostly Raw, Daiya cheese fits the bill. Or, if you who have a family member who doesn't want to travel down the vegan path with you... have him or her give this a try! It's so much healthier than animal-based cheese. For more information about Daiya's cheese, visit Daiyafoods.com.

2

•••

Partly Raw Recipes to Knock Your Socks Off!

Whenever we do what we can, we immediately can do more.

JAMES FREEMAN CLARKE

Nutty Breakfast Quinoa

Yield 1 large serving

Quinoa is a great staple in the vegan diet. Many people revere it as a "super-grain," although it's technically not even a grain. It's the seed of a leafy plant. Quinoa is a great source for complete and balanced protein. It also has iron, zinc, copper, B-vitamins, to name a few. Plus, it is gluten-free.

> 1 cup cooked quinoa
>
> ½ cup *Fun Milk* (see recipe below)
>
> 2 tablespoons raisins
>
> 1 tablespoon hemp seeds
>
> 1 tablespoon raw pumpkin seeds
>
> 1 tablespoon raw walnuts, chopped
>
> 1 tablespoon dried coconut, shredded and unsweetened
>
> pinch stevia (optional)

Stir all of the ingredients together in a bowl and enjoy.

If you're using freshly cooked quinoa, the dish will be warm. If you're using cold quinoa that you previously cooked, then you can warm this dish using your dehydrator by setting the temperature around 125 degrees F for about 30–45 minutes or so. Or, you can simply enjoy it cold.

Fun Milk

Yield 1 ½ cups

This milk is *crazy fun* because of its 1) *fruitiness* from the banana and 2) *creaminess* from hemp seeds and almond butter. Hemp is a powerfully nutritious food and I make it a point to consume it multiple times a week. It's great for the whole family and available at health food stores.

>   1 cup water
>   1 banana, peeled and chopped
>   1 tablespoon hemp seeds
>   1 tablespoon raw almond butter or other raw nut/seed
>   butter
>   pinch Himalayan crystal salt

Blend all of the ingredients until smooth.

Harvest Bounty

This is a recipe that is full of natural flavors, big in nutrition, and wonderful for the holidays (or any time of year).

> 3 cups beets, chopped
>
> 3 cups carrots, chopped
>
> 2 cups apple, diced
>
> 1 cup avocado, diced and gently packed
>
> ⅛ teaspoon cinnamon or pumpkin spice blend (or more to taste)
>
> Himalayan crystal salt to taste
>
> black pepper to taste

Steam the beets and carrots until fork tender. Place them in a large bowl and add the remaining ingredients. Gently toss everything together and serve immediately.

Sweet Coconut Oat Bars

See photo at KristensRaw.com/photos.

Yield 8–10 bars

1 cup rolled oats

¾ cup hemp seeds

½ cup dried coconut, shredded and unsweetened

½ cup dried mulberries or golden raisins

⅓ cup raw protein powder

¼ cup raw cacao nibs

½ cup raw coconut spread or coconut butter (see Appendix B)

½ cup raw agave nectar (or maple syrup)

1 teaspoon coconut extract

⅛ teaspoon nutmeg

Place the oats, hemp seeds, dried coconut, mulberries, protein powder, and nibs in a mixing bowl. Briefly stir the ingredients together, and set aside. Next, using a blender (or mini food processor, fitted with the "S" blade), process the coconut butter, agave, coconut extract and nutmeg together until smooth. Add this mixture to the bowl with rolled oats.

Mix thoroughly by hand, or as I prefer, use a mixer with the paddle attachment. Transfer the mixture onto a baking sheet lined with parchment paper. Mold it into a square or rectangle (it doesn't have to fit the whole pan). Refrigerate for an hour. Cut into bars and wrap them individually with parchment paper and then with plastic wrap. Store in the refrigerator or freezer.

"Give Me More!" Stuffed Bell Peppers

See photo at KristensRaw.com/photos.

Yield 4 cups stuffing (approximately 4–6 stuffed peppers)

The crisp crunch from the fresh bell pepper combined with the warmth of the brown rice and the "smoosh" factor from the avocado and soaked sun-dried tomatoes are absolutely delicious.

¼ cup raw sunflower seeds

½ cup sun-dried tomatoes

1 ½ cups cooked brown rice

1 cup spinach, chopped and gently packed

1 avocado, pitted, peeled, and diced

¼ cup fresh basil leaves, chopped

1 clove garlic, pressed

2 tablespoons green onion, chopped

1 tablespoon tamari (wheat-free)

1–2 teaspoons fresh lime juice

1 teaspoon cumin

¼ teaspoon ginger powder

dash nutmeg

4–6 yellow, red, or orange bell peppers

Place the sunflower seeds in a bowl and cover completely with water plus about an inch. Let them soak for 6–8 hours. Drain off the water and give them a quick rinse. Place the sun-dried tomatoes in a separate bowl and add enough water to cover them. Let them soak for up to an hour. Drain the water off.

When the seeds and sun-dried tomatoes are ready to use, set them aside in a large bowl together. Begin cooking the brown rice as directed by the manufacturer's instructions. While the rice is cooking, prepare the other ingredients and place them in the bowl with the sun-dried tomatoes. Add the (warm) cooked brown rice to the bowl and toss to mix.

Take your bell peppers and cut off the tops (including the stems). Dig out the seeded part. Spoon the stuffing into the bell peppers.

Rustic Country Breakfast

See photo at KristensRaw.com/photos.

Yield 6 cups

Do you want some old-fashioned comfort food... except super healthy? *This is it!* By adding the cooked potato along with the warmed kale and tomato, you really get an immediate *"I'm wrapped in a nice warm blanket"* feel.

    1 medium carrot, chopped

    1 yellow or red bell pepper, seeded and chopped

    1 ½ cups portabella mushrooms, chopped

    1 cup broccoli florets, chopped

    1 tablespoon tamari (wheat-free)

    1 tablespoon raw olive oil

    1–2 teaspoons fresh lime juice

    1 teaspoon dried marjoram

    1–3 tablespoons canola oil

    1 medium potato, (peeled if desired), chopped*

    1 Roma tomato, chopped

    2 leaves curly kale, destemmed, and chopped

    ⅓ cup Daiya™ cheddar vegan cheese**

    Himalayan crystal salt to taste

    black pepper to taste

Place the carrot, bell pepper, mushroom, and broccoli into a large bowl and stir to mix. Whisk the tamari, olive oil, lime juice and marjoram in a small bowl and pour over the vegetable mixture.

Toss to mix. *While you're preparing the rest of the recipe, be sure to come back and toss this mixture a few times to ensure all of the veggies are getting marinated.*

Heat a sauté pan to medium heat and add the canola oil. Let it warm for about 30–60 seconds. Add the potato and let it cook until fork tender, turning often (this could be anywhere from 10–15 minutes depending on the size of the pieces). Turn the heat off and remove the pan from heat. Add the tomatoes and kale and stir for about 30 seconds. Place the pan back on the burner that you turned off (keep it off, but you're going to use it now because it's still warm). Add the Daiya cheese and stir to mix. When the cheese begins to melt (within seconds), transfer the potato mixture to the large bowl with the Raw ingredients. Season with salt and pepper to taste. Enjoy immediately to experience the warm properties of the dish.

* For the potato, keep in mind that you want same-sized pieces to ensure they cook evenly. The smaller they are, the faster they'll cook.

** See information on Daiya vegan cheese, Ch. 1.

Tofu Eggless Salad

Yield 4 cups

I love this recipe because it's satisfying and easy to make. Tofu is a high-quality source of protein, and although I don't eat a lot of soy, I like having a few good recipes on hand. My husband loves this recipe and likes it in sandwiches or globbed onto a big spinach salad.

1 package (approximately 14 oz) extra firm tofu, diced

¼ cup vegan mayonnaise*

3 green onions, chopped (green part only)

4 small–medium radishes, minced

½ cup parsley, chopped

1 medium carrot, diced

2 tablespoons fresh basil leaves, minced

2 tablespoons hemp seeds (or more)

1 tablespoon yellow mustard (or Dijon if desired)

1 tablespoon fresh jalapeno, minced

¼ teaspoon garlic powder

¼ teaspoon Himalayan crystal salt (more if desired)

¼ teaspoon black pepper

Place all of the ingredients in a large bowl and stir. You can enjoy Tofu Eggless Salad plain or you can serve it (1 cup per serving or more) on top of a huge spinach salad with plenty of freshly chopped tomatoes. To that combination, you can also add a drizzle of olive oil and a splash of balsamic vinegar (or a squeeze of fresh citrus).

Another option is that you can serve the Tofu Eggless Salad stuffed inside a stemmed and seeded red, orange or yellow bell pepper... or stuffed inside a seeded tomato (get heirloom tomatoes if they're in season).

* My favorite brand is Veganaise™, the organic variety. This is available at many health food stores.

Kale-N-Rice

Yield 3–4 servings

Once people try a raw marinated kale salad, most of them become addicted. It's not unusual for our family to eat them a few times a week. These salads are also a fun way to get any skeptics excited about kale, and this recipe contains a nice, warm "smoosh" factor.

1 large bunch curly kale

¾–1 teaspoon Himalayan crystal salt

¼ teaspoon black pepper

⅛ teaspoon nutmeg

2 tablespoons fresh lemon or lime juice

2 ½ tablespoons raw olive or hemp oil

1 cup grapes, halved

¼ cup raisins

3–4 tablespoons raw sunflower seeds

2–3 cups cooked brown rice*

Destem the kale. You can leave the more tender parts of the stem (toward the top of each leaf) in the salad, but the harder stems toward the bottom of each leaf should be removed. Tear apart the kale leaves into bite-size pieces (or use a knife and chop them).

Place the torn kale in a large bowl. Add the salt, pepper, nutmeg, lemon juice, and oil. Take a minute and thoroughly massage all of these ingredients together with your hands (the kale shrinks as you do this). Add the grapes, raisins, and sunflower seeds and toss to mix. When you're done cooking the brown rice, add it (while still warm/hot) and toss to mix.

Variations:

- I encourage you to use whatever ingredients you have on hand. As long as you have the foundation (kale—or some other dark and hearty leafy green, along with salt, pepper, fresh citrus, oil, and brown rice, or some other cooked grain) then you're good to go.
- Add other ingredients based on what you have. A good rule of thumb is to include something sweet to help offset the bitterness of the kale (ex: raisins, chopped dates, sliced banana, diced orange, pineapple, mango).
- You might also add: olives, (soaked) sun-dried tomatoes, dried apricots, avocado, nuts/seeds, other dried fruits (cranberries, goji berries, etc), bell pepper (red, orange or yellow), carrot, celery, shallot or green onion, shredded coconut.

---

* The rice adds the warm smooshy component of making this an excellent Raw Vegan Transition recipe. However, this recipe can be made different ways for different audiences. If you are "more" into Raw, then you'll probably want to use less rice (maybe 1–2 cups). If you are not into Raw very much (yet!), then increase the amount of rice and use about 2–3 cups.

Atlantian Avocado Pasta

Yield 4 servings

This is a creamy and nutritious Raw, plant-based sauce that gets warm as it's tossed onto cooked pasta with bites of fresh tomatoes and flavor. This recipe is sensational. After I made it for the first time, I made it again within days... it's so good.

> 1 (16 oz) box pasta (any shape)

Tomato Corn Salsa

> 3 cups tomatoes, diced
>
> 1 cup fresh pineapple, diced
>
> ½ cup cilantro, chopped
>
> ½ cup fresh corn (or frozen and thawed)
>
> 1 tablespoon red onion, minced
>
> 1 teaspoon garlic, pressed
>
> ½ teaspoon Himalayan crystal salt
>
> ⅛ teaspoon cayenne pepper
>
> black pepper (to taste)

Avocado Sauce

> 3 medium avocados, pitted and peeled
>
> ½ cup water
>
> 1 ½ tablespoons fresh lime juice
>
> ½–¾ teaspoon chipotle seasoning (more or less to taste)

¼ teaspoon cumin

¼ teaspoon Himalayan crystal salt (or more to taste)

drizzle raw agave nectar (optional)

Cook the pasta according to the manufacturer's instructions. While the pasta is cooking, prepare the salsa and sauce.

To make the Tomato Corn Salsa, toss all of the ingredients together in a bowl. To make the Avocado Sauce, blend all of the ingredients in a blender until creamy.

Place the cooked pasta in a large bowl and add the salsa and sauce. Toss everything together gently until the noodles are coated with sauce. Taste it and add more salt and/or agave, if desired.

Tropical Non-Eggs Benedict

Yield 1 serving

Avocado makes a neat scrambled egg substitute because of the texture and relatively bland taste. However, avocado is certainly not mild when it comes to nutrition. It's filled with fiber and B-vitamins, including folic acid.

> 1 sprouted English muffin (toasted if desired)
> 2 slices pineapple, peeled, and cored
> Ginger Scrambled Avocado (recipe below)
> Sprouts (optional)

Ginger Scrambled Avocado

> 1 large avocado, pitted and peeled
> 1 teaspoon fresh lime juice
> ⅛ teaspoon ginger powder (or more)
> ⅛ teaspoon turmeric powder
> pinch Himalayan crystal salt
> pinch black pepper

Mash all of the Ginger Scrambled Avocado ingredients together in a bowl until they resemble scrambled eggs. Place a pineapple ring on each English muffin half. Scoop Ginger Scrambled Avocado on top and finish it off with sprouts, if desired.

Variation:

- Make this recipe Mediterranean style—Mediterranean Non-Eggs Benedict. Simply replace the pineapple with tomato slices. Then, replace the ginger powder with ¼ teaspoon dried basil and replace the lime juice with lemon juice.

Mesquite Granola

Yield 6–8 servings

I love making my own granola. This is a great example of a Raw lifestyle transitional recipe because you combine Raw cereal you make yourself with non-Raw plant-based milk you buy from the store (rice, hemp, almond, oat, hazelnut, soy, coconut, etc). When you're ready to make it All-Raw, simply whip up a batch of your own Raw Cashew Hemp Milk to enjoy with it (see recipe, Ch. 3).

> 1 cup dry raw buckwheat groats (see Appendix C)
>
> ½ cup raw sunflower seeds
>
> ½ cup hemp seeds
>
> 10 prunes, pitted, soaked 30 minutes, and drained
>
> 5 medjool dates, pitted, soaked 30 minutes, and drained
>
> ⅔ cup fresh orange juice
>
> 1 tablespoon mesquite powder
>
> 1 teaspoon vanilla extract
>
> dash Himalayan crystal salt

Soak your buckwheat groats per the instructions in Appendix C.

Place the sunflower seeds in a bowl and cover with water plus about an inch. Let soak for 6–8 hours. Drain off the water and give them a quick rinse.

Once the buckwheat groats and sunflower seeds are soaked and ready to go, place them in a large bowl, add the hemp seeds, and set aside. Blend the remaining ingredients and pour the blended mixture over the seed mixture. Stir it all together until all of the seeds and buckwheat are thoroughly coated.

Spread the mixture onto a dehydrator tray, fitted with a nonstick ParaFlexx sheet (these dehydrating instructions apply to Excalibur dehydrators. If you don't have one, then you can use parchment paper with your dehydrator). Dehydrate at 130 degrees F for about 65 minutes. Reduce the temperature to 105 degrees F and dehydrate another 10–12 hours.

Flip the granola onto a regular mesh tray without a ParaFlexx sheet and peel off the ParaFlexx sheet. Continue dehydrating until dry (approximately 12–24 hours). Break the granola into the desired size chunks or pieces that you want.

Plant Power Burgers

See photo on cover and at KristensRaw.com/photos.

Yield 3 burgers

These are awesome. When you put it all together with the sprouted bun, mustard, and other components, you'll never miss regular, greasy, artery-clogging burgers again. One of the best parts is that the burger is warm from the dehydrator even though the burger "meat" is RAW! These rock the house!

The Components

3 sprouted buns (available at the health food store)

3 tomato slices

3 romaine lettuce leaves

mustard

3 Plant Power Burger Patties

For the Plant Power Burger Patties

Yield 3 patties

2 cups portabella mushrooms, chopped

½ cup carrots, chopped

½ cup fresh basil leaves, gently packed

¼ cup + 2 tablespoons hemp seeds

3 tablespoons chia seeds

2–4 tablespoons water

1 ½ tablespoons raw sprouted brown rice protein powder
(plain flavored)

1 ½ tablespoons coconut aminos or wheat-free tamari

1 teaspoon onion powder

¼ teaspoon dried dill

⅛ teaspoon black pepper

Using a food processor, fitted with the "S" blade, process all of the ingredients until thoroughly combined. Transfer to a bowl and set aside for 15–20 minutes to thicken.

Make 3 patties using a round mold, or your hands, and place on a dehydrator tray. Dehydrate at 130–135 degrees F for 75 minutes. Reduce the temperature to 105–115 degrees F and continue dehydrating another 3–4 hours (or longer, if desired).

Place each Plant Power Burger Patty on a bun, top with mustard, tomato, and romaine lettuce. Enjoy!

Black-N-Blue Cobbler

My husband loves cobblers! I usually make them 100% Raw by omitting the Rapadura used below, but leaving it in makes this particular recipe a transitional, "mostly Raw" recipe. Black-N-Blue Cobbler will knock the socks off of any person who loves cooked food, even though most of the recipe is made from raw ingredients. This recipe is designed to be a dessert, but heck, I've eaten it for breakfast!

> 2 ½ cups raw pecans
>
> ¼ cup Rapadura sugar
>
> ½ teaspoon allspice
>
> ¼ teaspoon Himalayan crystal salt
>
> ½ cup dried coconut, shredded and unsweetened
>
> ½ cup raisins
>
> 2 (8–10oz) bags frozen blueberries, thawed and drained
>
> 1 (8–10oz) bag frozen blackberries, thawed and drained
>
> ¼ cup fresh orange juice
>
> 1 teaspoon vanilla extract

Using a food processor, fitted with the "S" blade, grind the pecans, Rapadura, allspice, and salt until you attain a medium-coarse grind. Add the coconut and raisins and process until combined and it begins to clump together a bit.

Place one bag of the thawed blueberries in a medium–large bowl and set aside. Using a blender, blend the second bag of blueberries along with the blackberries, orange juice, and vanilla. Pour the blended mixture over the whole blueberries in the bowl, and stir to mix.

Place ½–⅔ of the pecan mixture into an 8 × 8 glass baking dish and press down gently. Pour the berry mixture on top and spread out. Sprinkle the remainder of the pecan mixture on top. Serve and enjoy. Or, you can warm it in your dehydrator for 1–2 hours at 125 degrees F. Store leftover cobbler in the refrigerator, covered, for up to three days.

Fiesta Tostadas

See photo at KristensRaw.com/photos.

Yield 2 servings (4 tostadas)

Mexican tacos or tostadas can easily be made into a Raw Vegan Transition recipe. With the tostadas and beans as the only cooked ingredients, you enjoy a meal that is also loaded with Raw goodies and nutritionally superior to regular cooked tostadas. And in my opinion, better tasting, too!

½ cup black beans, dry, uncooked

4 corn tostadas

1 cup romaine lettuce, chopped or shredded

½–¾ cup Cheezy Hemp Nacho Sauce (see recipe, Ch. 4)

¾–1 cup Tomato Orange Salsa (see recipe, below)

½–⅔ cup Fiesta Guacamole (see recipe, below)

Sort out any black beans that look bad, broken (or if you see any stones), and throw them away. Take the remaining good black beans and rinse them well. Place them in a bowl covered with enough water by at least a couple of inches and let them soak for 6–8 hours. Drain the soaked beans.

Put the beans in a pot with enough water to cover the beans by a couple of inches, and bring to a boil. Reduce to a simmer and let cook for 2–3 hours, or until soft. Drain off excess water and set aside. Take a tostada and spread 1–2 tablespoons (or more) of Fiesta Guacamole on it. Top it with about ¼ cup of cooked black beans. Add some shredded lettuce, Tomato Orange Salsa, and then drizzle Cheezy Hemp Nacho Sauce on top. Delicious!

Tomato Orange Salsa

1 cup tomatoes, diced

1 orange, peeled, segmented, seeded, and diced

¼ cup cilantro leaves

½ teaspoon fresh orange zest

⅛ teaspoon paprika

pinch Himalayan crystal salt

pinch black pepper

Toss all of the ingredients together in a bowl.

Fiesta Guacamole

2 avocados, pitted and peeled

½ cup carrots, shredded

1 ½ teaspoons fresh lime juice

¼ teaspoon cumin

⅛ teaspoon Himalayan crystal salt

pinch black pepper

Place all of the ingredients in a bowl and mash together.

Quick Wrap Sandwich with Kristen's Ultimate Raw Spread

Yield 2 servings

This is one fast, easy, and delicious recipe. You can have it as a lunch or snack. And, to take it to the next level as an All-Raw recipe, simply replace the whole-wheat tortillas with Raw foods. For example, I love using big leaves of romaine lettuce and slathering this spread onto it—yum! Or, spread it in celery stalks. You can also seed a cucumber and fill it up with the spread.

> 4 whole-wheat tortillas
>
> 2 cups romaine lettuce, chopped
>
> ¾–1 cup Kristen's Ultimate Raw Spread (recipe below)

Spread about 3–4 tablespoons of Kristen's Ultimate Raw Spread on each whole-wheat tortilla and top with lettuce. You can have fun and add all kinds of different raw toppings to this such as freshly chopped tomatoes, shredded carrots, minced olives, sliced cucumber, sprouts, etc. Having variety like this makes living the Raw lifestyle seriously *fun*.

Kristen's Ultimate Raw Spread

Yield 2 cups

¾ cup raw cashews

2 cups sun-dried tomatoes

⅔ cup hemp seeds

½ cup of the reserved soak water from the sun-dried
   tomatoes, more if needed

2 tablespoons onion, chopped

1 tablespoon tamari, wheat-free

1 tablespoon light miso

1 tablespoon dried basil

⅛–¼ teaspoon black pepper

Place the cashews in a bowl and cover with water plus about an inch. Let them soak for 1 hour. Drain off the water and give them a quick rinse. Place the sun-dried tomatoes in a separate bowl and add enough water to cover them. Let them soak for up to an hour. Drain the water off into another bowl and keep it for use later in the recipe.

When the cashews and sun-dried tomatoes are ready to use, place them in a blender with the remaining ingredients. Blend everything until creamy.

Double Chocolate Almond Chia Pudding

Yield 2–3 servings

One of the beauties of this recipe is making it quickly with a carton of non-dairy (plant-based) milk from the store. Talk about easy!

⅓ cup chia seeds

2 tablespoons raw cacao nibs

¾ cup non-dairy milk from the store

1 tablespoon raw agave nectar (optional, depending on the sweetness of the non-dairy milk used)

2 tablespoons raw chocolate powder

⅛ teaspoon almond extract

Place the chia seeds and the cacao nibs in a small to medium bowl and briefly toss to mix. Use a blender to blend the remaining ingredients together. Then, pour the blended mixture over the chia seed mixture, and stir to mix.

Wait a few minutes and stir again. (You'll notice the chia seeds beginning to take on a gelatinous texture.) Wait a few minutes, again, and stir. Place the Double Chocolate Almond Chia Pudding in the refrigerator for 15–20 minutes (or longer, if desired). However, if you can't wait (like me), then simply start eating it right away.

"OMG" Chickpea Salad

The first time I made this I gave a serving to my husband. He loved it and cleaned his bowl, then asked for more. I had a serving myself so there were two servings left that I put in a bowl in the refrigerator for later. I took the bowl and just gave it to him with another fork and said, "Eat what you want and put the rest back when you're done." Um. He finished the whole thing, which means he had *three servings in a row!*

    1 cup red quinoa, cooked

    2 cups chickpeas (canned or cooked)*

    2 cups grape tomatoes (or cherry tomatoes), halved

    2 cups zucchini, chopped

    1 tablespoon hemp seeds

    ¾–1 cup Ginger Shallot Dressing (see recipe, Ch. 4)

Toss everything in a bowl gently.

---

* If you use canned chickpeas, rinse them well before adding them to the salad so you can remove some of the excess sodium.

Fresh Summer Marinara and Pasta

Yield 3–4 servings

Sometimes when people eat Raw vegan pasta for the first time (meaning the noodles are made from veggies like zucchini or cucumbers) with raw marinara, they have a hard time getting over the "coldness" of it. It doesn't always give you that familiar pasta comfort-food experience with which you've grown up. That's where this recipe becomes a great Raw Vegan Transition recipe. Beware though: The marinara is so delicious that you might eat it right out of the food processor and not have any left for the pasta. Been there, done that!

Tips for how this becomes comfort-food-like in experience: The heat from the noodles will help warm the sauce a bit, making it more of a room temperature food, convincing even the most skeptical. Furthermore, you can use ingredients to make the marinara that are at room temperature. Think about that ahead of time when making this and if something is in the refrigerator, like the bell pepper, take it out before making the marinara to reach room temperature.

> ¾ cup sun-dried tomatoes
>
> 3 medium tomatoes (about 3 cups chopped)
>
> 1 red, orange, or yellow bell pepper, seeded and chopped
>
> 2 green onions (green and white parts), chopped
>
> 7 sun-dried olives, pitted*
>
> ⅓ cup fresh basil leaves, gently packed

⅓ cup fresh Italian (flat leaf) parsley, gently packed

2 tablespoons raw olive oil

1 tablespoon balsamic vinegar

1 teaspoon Italian seasoning

1 clove garlic, minced

¼ teaspoon Himalayan crystal salt

⅛ teaspoon black pepper

1 (16 oz) box of noodles

Place the sun-dried tomatoes in a bowl and add enough water to cover them. Let them soak for up to an hour. Drain the water off.

When the sun-dried tomatoes are ready, place all of the ingredients (except the noodles) in a food processor, fitted with the "S" blade, and pulse the mixture until you reach your desired texture. I prefer mine slightly chunky so I can still see all of the gorgeous vibrant colors. Processing it too long will make it all one color.

Prepare the noodles according to the manufacturer's directions. After you've portioned out the noodles into serving bowls, top each bowl of noodles with the sauce.

* To pit the olives, place them on a clean surface. Using a spatula (or food scraper), simply press down on them. It cracks the skin and the pits are easy to extract.

Perfect Potato Salad

Yield approximately 10–12 cups

Perfect Potato Salad makes a lot and that's okay! Between my husband and me, we usually polish it off in three days. And, when I'm feeling generous, I send my husband to work with some to share with his clients. What better way to introduce people to vegan food (and get them hooked!)?

Veggie Salad Mixture

- 2 pounds red skin potatoes
- olive oil (to drizzle)
- 1 red bell pepper, seeded and diced
- corn cut from 2 cobs*
- 1 cup parsley, chopped
- ½ cup cilantro, chopped
- ½ cup hemp seeds
- 3 stalks celery, chopped
- 2 medium carrots, thinly sliced with a mandoline (or shredded)
- 1 zucchini, diced

Dressing Ingredients

- 1 cup vegan mayonnaise**
- 3 tablespoons yellow mustard
- 2 teaspoons Himalayan crystal salt

½ teaspoon black pepper

2 green onions (white and green parts), chopped

¼ cup fresh basil leaves, minced

2 teaspoons fresh orange zest

1 teaspoon fresh lemon zest

Preheat the oven to 350 degrees F. Wash and cut the potatoes into bite-sized pieces (cut them evenly, if possible, so they bake evenly). Put them in a bowl, drizzle a little olive oil on them and toss to lightly coat. Place the potatoes on a baking sheet (the kind of baking sheet with a little lip on the edge works best), and spread them out if possible.

Bake the potatoes until fork tender (approximately 35–55 minutes, depending on the size). While they're baking, prepare the rest of the veggies and put them in a large bowl. When the potatoes are done cooking, take them out of the oven and add them to the veggie bowl.

Stir the dressing ingredients together in a medium bowl and add this to the bowl with all of the veggies. Gently toss to mix everything together.

Variations:

- Try adding olives, raisins, sprouts, capers, sea veggies, and/or other herbs. So delicious!

---

* Raw corn cut right off the cob tastes amazing. To make sure you have this year round, stock up on organic corn on the cob when it's in season. Cut the corn from the cobs and freeze.

** My favorite brand is Veganaise™, the organic option. This is available at many health food stores.

Miso's Lentils

Yield 2 servings

This is a snuggly comfort recipe that's perfect for chilly winter days. Miso's Lentils gives you an easy way to sneak super healthy kale to your family's life.

> 1 cup dry red lentils
>
> 2 cups water
>
> 1–1 ½ tablespoons miso (more if desired)
>
> ½ cup sun-dried tomatoes, broken into pieces if possible
>
> black pepper to taste
>
> 2 medium–large dinosaur kale leaves, destemmed, and chopped into bite size pieces
>
> 2 small handfuls of raisins

Rinse the lentils well. Place them in a quart-size pot with the water and bring to a boil. Lower the heat, cover the pot, and allow them to simmer for 20–25 minutes. Remove from heat, uncover and allow to set for about 5 minutes to help the lentils to cool off a bit. Stir in the miso and sun-dried tomatoes. Season with black pepper to taste. Place the kale and raisins in two bowls. Pour lentils on top and stir to mix.

Variations:

- You can change this recipe by adding nuts, seeds, carrots, jicama, bell pepper, zucchini, or celery. Try different herbs and spices, too.

Power Quinoa

Yield approximately 4 cups

Are you looking for some extra protein in your diet? Quinoa fits the bill. I'm a fan of quinoa because it's versatile and offers great nutrients. The sauerkraut kicks the nutrition of this recipe up a huge notch, too.

> 2 cups cooked quinoa
>
> 1 red bell pepper, seeded and diced
>
> 1 avocado, pitted, peeled and diced
>
> ½ cup celery, chopped
>
> ¼ cup raw, unpasteurized sauerkraut (or more)
>
> 2 tablespoons fresh basil leaves, minced
>
> 1 ½ green onions (green part only), minced
>
> Himalayan crystal salt to taste
>
> black pepper to taste

Gently toss all of the ingredients together in a bowl.

Variations:

- Try other mix-ins, such as carrots, broccoli, cucumber, mushrooms, pineapple, apple, grapes, beets (raw or steamed), or zucchini.

Savory Garden Vegetables with Buckwheat Noodles

See photo at KristensRaw.com/photos.

Yield 3 servings

The Marinade Ingredients

½ cup raw olive oil

2 tablespoons tamari, wheat-free

juice of 1 lemon

2 cloves garlic, pressed

1 teaspoon onion powder

½ teaspoon garlic powder

¼ teaspoon mustard powder

2 pinches black pepper

The Vegetable Mixture Ingredients

2 cups carrots, sliced*

1 head broccoli florets, chopped

1 red bell pepper, seeded and diced

1 yellow bell pepper, seeded and diced

12 ounces buckwheat soba noodles**

Directions for the Marinade

Whisk all of the ingredients together and set aside while you prepare the vegetables.

Directions for the Vegetables

Prepare the vegetables and place in a large bowl. Pour the marinade over the vegetables and toss well to coat. Allow the marinade to work its magic on the vegetables by helping to soften them for about 30 minutes (or longer if desired). Also, you can place the bowl of marinating vegetables in a dehydrator for 25–30 minutes set at 130 degrees F.

Directions for the Noodles

Prepare the noodles according to the directions. Once they're prepared, place them in individual serving bowls and top with the marinated vegetables. (For extra mojo, sprinkle on some hemp seeds and raisins!)

Variations:

- When you are ready to take this magnificent dish to the All-Raw level, swap out the buckwheat noodles for fresh zucchini, carrot, beet, and/or cucumber noodles. It's a nutritious meal with tons of flavor!

---

* I love using my mandoline to slice the carrots. It's fun to have different shapes of vegetables. However, if you don't have a mandoline, you can simply chop the carrots.

** You can use a variety of noodles, but I love this recipe with organic buckwheat soba noodles. The brand I usually buy at Whole Foods Market is O'Hana House (in the refrigerated section).

Vegan Pepperoni Pizza

See photo at KristensRaw.com/photos.

Yield one 8-inch pizza

Raw pizza recipes, for some people, can be like Raw pasta recipes: kind of weird, unfamiliar, and disappointingly different from the expected (and much-loved) cooked version. This recipe is a terrific transition recipe, because you get the yumminess of a real cooked crust, but the rest of the pizza is loaded with flavor, texture, and nutrition, from raw ingredients. You'll be amazed at how the raw sauerkraut acts as a super replacement for cheese and the raw vegan pepperoni recipe is so cool it's mind-blowing!

The Sauce Ingredients

2 cups tomatoes, chopped

1 ½ cups red bell pepper, seeded and chopped

¼ cup fresh basil leaves, packed

1 medium clove garlic, pressed

1 teaspoon fresh lemon juice

½ teaspoon dried oregano

¼ teaspoon Himalayan crystal salt

⅛ teaspoon kelp powder or granules

pinch black pepper

The Toppings

¼ cup Raw, unpasteurized sauerkraut

3–4 olives, pitted and chopped

10 slices Raw Vegan Pepperoni (recipe below)

The Crust

One 8-inch pizza crust (see details, below)

Directions for the Sauce

Using a food processor, fitted with the "S" blade, process all of the ingredients until you have a texture that is just slightly chunky, but sauce-like. Place the sauce in a strainer over a bowl (to drain off excess liquid), while you prepare the rest of the ingredients.

Directions for the Crust

You can prepare your own crust from scratch, or buy one that is pre-made and needs to be heated (pre-made is much easier!). The crust I buy is from Whole Foods Market. The brand is Vicolo and they make an organic spelt and cornmeal crust that comes two in a package. Cook the crust according to the manufacturer's directions or according to your own homemade recipe if you're making your own.

TIP: While the crust is cooking, have the sauce and sauerkraut in two glass bowls sitting on top of the oven (NOT "in" the oven, just in bowls on "top" of the oven, assuming your oven is below your stovetop). The reason for this is the oven gives off heat, which can help take the chill off those ingredients.

Directions for the Assembly

Once the crust is cooked, take it out of the oven and immediately spread the sauce on it. Then, put the sauerkraut on top of the sauce, covering the entire pizza evenly (as though it were grated cheese). Next, place the olives and pepperoni slices on top.

Raw Vegan Pepperoni

Yield 15–20 pepperoni slices measuring about 1 ¼ inch in diameter

This is simply my Cheezy Hemp Nacho Sauce (see recipe, Ch. 4) that I love to make ALL THE TIME. Only this time, the recipe is basically cut in half and dehydrated. Yes, that's right... a dehydrated cheezy sauce makes wonderful vegan mock-pepperoni!

> 3 tablespoons water
>
> 1 small clove garlic
>
> 1 tablespoon fresh lemon juice
>
> ½ cup red bell pepper, seeded and chopped
>
> ½ cup hemp seeds
>
> 1 ¼ tablespoons nutritional yeast flakes
>
> 1 ½ teaspoons chili powder*
>
> 1 teaspoon tamari, wheat-free
>
> ¼ teaspoon Himalayan crystal salt
>
> ¼ teaspoon garlic powder
>
> ⅛ teaspoon cayenne pepper
>
> pinch turmeric powder

Blend all of the ingredients in a blender until smooth and creamy. Spread the mixture onto a dehydrator tray lined with a non-stick ParaFlexx sheet. Dehydrate at 105 degrees F for 12–24 hours, or until you can flip the mixture onto a regular dehydrator tray and peel off the non-stick ParaFlexx sheet.

Once it is flipped, continue dehydrating another 8–12 hours, or until you get a texture that is like a flexible-solid feel. Transfer this to a counter top and use a round cookie cutter measuring about 1¼ inch in diameter and cut the pepperoni circles. Gobble up the left over dehydrated mixture after the circles have been cut (or crumble it over your next salad—it reminds my stepdad of bacon bits).

* My favorite brand for this is Simply Organic™. I highly recommend using this brand for the best flavor.

Hemp Pesto Pizza

Yield one 8-inch pizza

The basil flavor in this recipe is so delicious that you'll find your-self eating slower so you can savor each and every bite. I bet any-one that you make this recipe for is going to love it.

The Components

1 8-inch pizza crust (see "Crust Options," below)

½ cup tomatoes, seeded and diced

Marinated mushrooms (see recipe, below)

Basil Hempy Pesto (see recipe, below)

For the Marinated Mushrooms

¾ cup mushrooms, sliced

2 teaspoons olive oil

2 teaspoons tamari, wheat-free

pinch black pepper

For the Basil Hempy Pesto

3 cups fresh basil leaves, gently packed

½ cup hemp seeds

2 cloves garlic, pressed

1 teaspoon fresh squeezed lemon juice

½ teaspoon Himalayan crystal salt

⅓ cup olive oil

Crust Options

You can make your own crust from scratch, or buy one that is premade and needs to be heated. The crust I usually buy is from Whole Foods Market. The brand is *Vicolo* and they make an organic spelt and cornmeal crust that comes two in a package. Cook the crust according to the manufacturer's directions or according to your own homemade recipe if you're making your own.

Directions for the Mushrooms

Place the mushrooms in a bowl with the other ingredients and toss to coat. Set aside while you make the pesto.

Directions for the Basil Hempy Pesto

Since the pesto is quite simple and fast to prepare, I recommend getting your crust cooking while you make the pesto so that it is vibrantly fresh when placed on top of the pizza.

Place all of the ingredients, except the olive oil, into a food processor, fitted with the "S" blade and process. While the food processor is running, add the olive oil in a steady stream. Once all of the oil is incorporated, turn off the food processor.

Directions for the Assembly

Take the pizza crust out of the oven. Spread the pesto on top of the crust. Top with the chopped tomatoes. Before adding the mushrooms, gently squeeze them so you can remove some of the wetness.

Disco Lima Bean Mash

Yield 3 cups

I've always been a fan of lima beans, but since eating a mostly Raw diet, I found that I was not having them very often. Not anymore though... I created this recipe so I could enjoy my lima beans while still getting plenty of healthy Raw nutrients and healthy fats. Move over mashed potatoes. It's time for some *Disco Lima Bean Mash!*

> 1 (10 oz) package frozen lima beans
>
> 3 cups zucchini, chopped
>
> ¼ cup raw cashew butter
>
> ¼ cup raw tahini
>
> 2 tablespoons Garlic Red Pepper Miso*
>
> 1 tablespoon fresh lime juice
>
> ¾ teaspoon garlic powder
>
> ⅛ teaspoon black pepper

Cook the lima beans according to the manufacturer's directions on the package. Place the remaining ingredients in a blender, add the cooked lima beans, and blend until you get a puree.

* You can use any miso, but this is one of my favorites. See Appendix B for details.

Caribbean Buckwheat

Yield approximately 3 servings

Each bite of this recipe reminds me of a tropical paradise. Hhmmmm! I love eating this for breakfast and then later again in the day for a hearty and nutritious snack. The goods on buckwheat: It has protein, fiber, B-vitamins, calcium, and more. Then, the raw ingredients in this recipe give you plenty of antioxidants, fiber, and tasty goodness.

The Sauce Ingredients

¼ cup raw cashews

1 young Thai coconut, meat and water*

½ teaspoon allspice

½ teaspoon vanilla extract

pinch Himalayan crystal salt

The Buckwheat/Fruit Mixture Ingredients

1 cup dry raw buckwheat groats

1 ½ cups pineapple, diced

1 cup mango, diced

1 banana, diced

Directions for the Sauce

Place the cashews in a bowl and cover with enough water by about an inch. Let them soak for 1 hour. Drain off the water and give them a quick rinse.

When the cashews are ready, use a blender to blend all of the sauce ingredients together until smooth. Transfer the sauce to a large bowl.

Directions for the Buckwheat

Rinse the buckwheat well. Combine the buckwheat with 2 cups of water and bring to a boil. Reduce the heat, cover, and simmer for about 25 minutes. While the buckwheat is cooking, prepare the fruit ingredients and add the fruit to the bowl with the sauce. When the buckwheat is done cooking, add the buckwheat to the bowl with the fruit and sauce. Stir everything together.

* For a video demonstration on how to open a young Thai coconut, visit my blog at: KristensRaw.blogspot.com/2010/02/how-to-open-young-thai-coconut-video.html

Warming Miso Soup with Raw Vegetables

Yield 2 servings

Miso is considered a "living" food (not Raw), because of its digestive elements. Miso soup is nutritious, warming, and wonderful for days when it's cold outside or if you feel under the weather. The rest of this dish is comprised of raw veggies, making it a nice Raw Vegan Transition dish. I like to have this for my lunch alongside raw organic flax crackers, spread with a delectable raw vegan cheese spread.

> **3 cups hot water**
>
> **1 tablespoon (or more) miso**
>
> **1 cup zucchini, spiralized into noodles***
>
> **½ cup red bell pepper, diced**
>
> **⅓ cup carrots, thinly sliced into rounds**
>
> **¼ cup oyster mushrooms, sliced**
>
> **1 tablespoon green onion, chopped**

Heat the water on your stove to very warm, but do not let it boil. Turn off the heat and stir in the miso. Divide the chopped vegetables into two serving bowls. Pour the miso broth on top.

---

* I use a Benriner vegetable turning slicer to make noodles from zucchini and other vegetables. Details available at KristensRaw.com/store. If you don't have a turning slicer you can use a vegetable peeler to make wide fettuccini style noodles.

Cheezy Corkscrew Macaroni— Kid Approved!

See photo at KristensRaw.com/photos.

Yield approximately 4–6 servings

Have you or your family been going without macaroni and cheese since you went vegan because you couldn't find a healthy (and tasty) enough animal-free substitute? Well, look no more. Here is a great Raw Vegan Transition recipe that you and your family are sure to enjoy. (I make this regularly for my parents and husband—it's one of their favorite dishes).

Be sure to get corkscrew noodles if you are feeding this to kids because they're fun, and they do a great job of holding sauce in their little crevices.

The Macaroni Ingredients

1 (16 oz) box of corkscrew noodles

The Sauce Ingredients

¾ cup raw cashews

¼ cup hemp seeds

½ cup water

1 red bell pepper, seeded and chopped

3 tablespoons tamari (wheat-free)*

3 tablespoons nutritional yeast

3 tablespoons fresh lemon juice

1 teaspoon onion powder

½ teaspoon turmeric powder

Place the cashews in a bowl and cover with water plus about an inch. Let them soak for 1 hour. Drain off the water and give them a quick rinse.

Prepare the noodles by boiling them according to the manufacturer's instructions. Blend the cashews and remaining sauce ingredients until smooth and pour on top of the cooked noodles. Toss the noodles and sauce to thoroughly mix.

NOTE: Did you know that you could use your blender to warm some Raw recipes without destroying the nutrients? This is a great trick and I like doing it for the sauce in this recipe. Simply blend the sauce an extra minute; the friction of the motion will make it warm. But be sure not to let it blend so long that it gets too hot.

Ready to make this even healthier? Add a bunch of chopped veggies to the mix such as diced tomatoes, zucchini, broccoli (lightly steamed or raw), and/or mushrooms.

Want to add some cooked vegan protein? Sauté four Gardein (vegan) chicken breasts, dice them up and stir into the final mixture. Amazing! This will please even your most die-hard carnivores.

Ready to make this recipe All-Raw? Use raw zucchini noodles in place of the cooked pasta. If you blend the sauce a bit longer for the warmth factor I mentioned in the note above, and if you use room temperature zucchini for the noodles, it will make it more of a comfort food even though it is All-Raw.

---

* I usually use "reduced sodium" tamari.

Protein Pesto Pasta

See photo at KristensRaw.com/photos.

Yield approximately 4 servings

When I gave the photographer this dish to photograph, it was funny because he handed it back to me half-eaten. Thankfully he took the photo before he started gobbling away at it.

>   1 (16 oz) box of noodles
>   3 cups tomatoes, diced

The Pesto Ingredients

>   2 cups fresh basil leaves, packed
>   ½ cup hemp seeds
>   1 teaspoon fresh lemon juice
>   1 teaspoon garlic, chopped
>   1 teaspoon balsamic vinegar
>   ½ teaspoon Himalayan crystal salt (more to taste)
>   ½ teaspoon fresh lemon zest
>   ⅛ teaspoon black pepper
>   ½ cup raw olive oil

Prepare the noodles according to the manufacturer's instructions. Place the cooked noodles in a large bowl and add the diced tomatoes. To prepare the pesto, use a food processor, fitted with the "S" blade, and briefly combine all of the ingredients except for the olive oil. As the food processor is running, pour the olive oil in as a steady stream. Do not over process. Add the pesto to the noodle mixture and gently toss.

Variation:

- As you transition to more Raw, replace some of the noodles with extra vegetables.

Spinach Ranch Tofu Salad

Yield 2 large servings

The first time I threw this together for my husband, he went bananas for it. He loved it and kept telling me how satisfying it was. Another great thing about it is that I can whip this together in about 15 minutes.

> 2 tablespoons canola oil or olive oil
>
> 1 (10 oz) package extra (or super) firm tofu, cubed*
>
> Juice from 1 lemon or lime
>
> 2 tablespoons tamari, wheat-free
>
> 1 (5 oz) bag of spinach
>
> 1 orange, red, or yellow bell pepper, seeded and chopped
>
> ½ cucumber, chopped
>
> 2 tablespoons raisins or diced prunes
>
> 6–8 tablespoons 60-Second Raw Ranch dressing (see recipe, Ch. 4)

Heat a sauté pan to medium heat. Add the oil and let the oil heat for 30 seconds. Add the cubed tofu. Let it cook for about a minute, and add the lemon juice and tamari. Stir and cook this for 5–7 minutes on medium heat. Divide the spinach between two serving plates. Add the bell pepper, cucumber, and raisins. Put the warm tofu on top. Add the dressing. Dive in!

* I buy organic, non-GMO tofu. One of my favorite brands is *Wild Wood Organics*. It comes packaged without much water (kind of shrink wrapped), so I can use it right away (there is no need to press and drain it).

Snazzy Root Soup

Yield 4 cups

This soup is awesome! It's vibrant, nutritious, and satisfying.

½ cup raw cashews

1 cup yam, peeled and chopped

1 cup carrot, peeled and chopped

1 cup beet, peeled and chopped

1 cup zucchini, peeled and chopped

½ cup + 2 tablespoons water (a little more if needed)

½ cup fresh orange juice

1 teaspoon fresh orange zest

1 teaspoon dried sage powder

¼ teaspoon Himalayan crystal salt

⅛ teaspoon black pepper

Place the cashews in a bowl and cover with water plus about an inch. Let them soak for 1 hour. Drain off the water and give them a quick rinse.

Steam the yam, carrot, and beet until slightly fork tender, about 4–8 minutes, depending on the size of the chunks you chopped. (The beet might take a minute longer than the other root vegetables.) Use a blender to blend the steamed vegetables with the rest of the ingredients until smooth.

Strawberry Chocolate Ginger Shake

Yield 4 cups

This is a delightful treat. Most often I drink the whole thing myself because I can't bring myself to share it.

> 1 ½ cups Vanilla Coconut Milk*
>
> 1 heaping cup ice
>
> 2 cups strawberries, diced
>
> 2 tablespoons hemp seeds
>
> 2 tablespoons raw chocolate powder
>
> 1 tablespoon fresh ginger, grated
>
> 1 tablespoon maple syrup

Blend all of the ingredients together.

* So Delicious™ makes this and you can find it in the refrigerated section of many health food stores. If you can't find it, substitute with any plant-based milk (rice, soy, etc.).

Coffee House Transition

Yield 1 serving

Enjoy coffee... *without the coffee!* This recipe has satisfied my coffee cravings many times. The instant this delicious concoction touches my tongue, my body does a little happy dance, and I smile from ear to ear. It's a much healthier recipe than what you'll get at a coffee house because it has Raw vegan nut milk in it, not to mention the "coffee aspect" is herbal and non-acidic.

> 1 ½–2 cups brewed Teeccino™*
>
> 1 cup raw nut/seed milk (see Raw Cashew Hemp Milk Ch. 3)
>
> 1 cup ice
>
> sweetener, such as raw agave nectar or stevia, if desired

Blend all of the ingredients together or put the ice in a glass and add the Teeccino™ and nut milk. Stir it up.

* For details about Teeccino™, see Appendix B. If you don't want to use Teeccino, you can substitute it with organic coffee (regular or decaf). However, keep in mind that Teeccino is alkalizing and healthier than coffee. And it tastes great!

Velvet Wine Sauce

Yield 2 ¼ cups

This is by far one of my favorite sauces. In fact, I love showing it off to others (especially people who aren't particularly into Raw, because it'll blow their minds at how delicious this is). Some people tell me it reminds them of cream of mushroom soup, others tell me it reminds them of cream of chicken soup, and I think it's like a cheese fondue my mom used to make when I was a kid. What will it remind you of?

    2 cups raw cashews
    3 tablespoons nutritional yeast
    1 cup water
    1 tablespoon tamari, wheat free
    1 ½ tablespoons white wine
    1 teaspoon onion powder

Place the cashews in a bowl and cover with enough water plus an inch. Let them soak for 1–2 hours. Drain off the water and rinse them. Transfer the cashews to a blender and add the remaining ingredients. Blend everything until smooth, velvety, and warm (about a minute).

Raw Vegan Transition serving suggestions:

- Serve this slathered all over toasted whole grain bread.

- After making the sauce, stir it into a bowl of cooked pasta (16oz box).
- Use as a fondue dipping sauce with steamed vegetables.
- Dip baked organic corn chips in it for a satisfying snack.

All Raw serving suggestions:

- Use as a delectable dip for different raw veggies (broccoli never tasted so good!)
- Pour over kelp noodles and enjoy. (To prepare kelp noodles: rinse them thoroughly and then put them in a bowl with the juice of one lemon or lime squeezed into it. Add enough water to cover the noodles and allow them to set like this for about an hour. Rinse thoroughly again. Voila! Ready to eat.)
- This can be enjoyed as a rich, creamy soup.

3
• • •

Sneaky Transition Recipes (They'll Never Know!)

Life is not merely to be alive, but to be well.

MARCUS VALERIUS MARTIAL

When you look over the recipes in this chapter, you might find yourself thinking, "Hey, wait a minute, Kristen — these recipes aren't Raw... they're normal food!" Exactly! That's the whole idea. You'd be mostly correct (these recipes have been tweaked a little from their standard everyday versions to make them extra yummy and nutritious). One of the best ways to introduce more Raw foods into your family's diet is to use what I call "Sneaky" Raw recipes. These are everyday foods and recipes that can be mostly Raw (or All Raw) that people are already accustomed to but that might not realize they're Raw! In this way, you can start gradually ramping up the percentage of Raw in your family's diet without setting off alarm bells. Remember, the more Raw people eat, the more their palates will adjust and the more receptive they'll be to new, less familiar Raw foods.

The following recipes are great for easing your family into a more Raw lifestyle, by gradually exposing their palates to Raw flavors and textures, but without abandoning the familiarity of certain cooked elements. They are also EASY and FAST to make!

Raw Cashew Hemp Milk with Boxed Cereal

Yield 2 cups milk

This is a great way to help your family transition away from cows' dairy without anybody realizing it because they'll be having their new plant-based milk with normal boxed cereal.

¼ cup raw cashews

1 ⅓ cups water

¼ cup hemp seeds

1 tablespoon raw agave nectar or 1–2 pitted dates

⅛ teaspoon almond extract

Place the cashews in a bowl and cover with water plus about an inch. Let them soak for 1 hour. Drain off the water and give them a quick rinse.

When the cashews are ready, blend all of the ingredients until smooth. Raw Cashew Hemp Milk will stay fresh for up to five days when stored in the refrigerator in an airtight container (glass mason jars are great). Pour on top of your favorite boxed cereal from the store (preferably one that is organic, without refined sugar).

Corn Chips & Spring Green Guacamole

Yield 2 cups guacamole

Chips and guacamole is a great Raw Transition snack or meal. The Raw guacamole is nutritious (add fresh salsa and it's even more Raw!). For the chips, the best way to go is organic, non-GMO (*baked, not fried*—if possible). When you're ready to take this up a notch to All-Raw, simply replace the corn chips with fresh veggies or make your own Raw corn chips.

Spring Green Guacamole

> 4 avocados, pitted and peeled
>
> 1 green onion, chopped (green part only)
>
> 1 ½ tablespoons fresh lime juice
>
> 1 ½ teaspoons dried dill
>
> ¼ teaspoon Himalayan crystal salt
>
> ⅛ teaspoon black pepper

Place all of the ingredients in a bowl and smash together with a fork or potato masher. Serve with your favorite organic corn chips (or veggies).

Coconut (or Soy) Yogurt with Superfood Raw Fixin's

Yield 1 serving

This is a tasty treat that can be eaten for breakfast, as a snack, or even for dessert. This recipe is easy and versatile, which makes it fun.

- 1 single serving container of vegan yogurt
- 1 banana, peeled and sliced
- 1 tablespoon hemp seeds
- 1 tablespoon raw cacao nibs
- 1 tablespoon goji berries

Stir all of the ingredients together in a bowl.

Variations:

- Experiment with adding some of the following variations: fruit (orange, mango, apple, or pineapple), sunflower seeds, pumpkin seeds, chopped walnuts or pecans, shredded coconut, and dried fruits (raisins, cranberries, cherries, or diced apricots).
- Take this to the next level and make it All-Raw by making your own Creamy Raw Vegan Yogurt (see recipe, Ch. 4).

Nut Butter & Raw Jam Sandwich

Yield 1 serving

Who doesn't love a nut butter and jam sandwich? Here's a great way to transition into a healthier version of it by using a *Raw* nut butter and a *Raw* jam with healthy sprouted bread. It's time to say "no" to icky, heart-clogging hydrogenated nut butters and sugary processed jams.

The Components

> 1–3 tablespoons Strawberry Chia Jam (see below)
>
> 1–3 tablespoons raw nut or seed butter (see below)
>
> 2 slices healthy, sprouted bread (see below)

Strawberry Chia Jam

Yield 1 ¼ cups

> 2 tablespoons chia seeds
>
> 2 cups strawberries, chopped*
>
> ¼ cup fresh orange juice

Place the chia seeds in a bowl and set aside. Briefly pulse the strawberries and orange juice in a blender (keep it a little chunky). Pour the strawberry mixture into the bowl with the chia seeds and stir to mix. Wait about 5–10 minutes and stir again. Repeat this process 1–2 more times until it is jam-like and the chia seeds have absorbed the excess liquid.

For Raw Nut or Seed Butter

You can buy Raw nut or seed butter from your health food store. There are different varieties such as hemp, almond, pecan, cashew, walnut, macadamia, and more. Some excellent brands are *Living Tree Community*, *Rejuvenative Brands*, and *Artisana*.

For the Healthy Sprouted Bread

You can buy healthy sprouted breads at the health food store. A couple of brands I like are *Good for Life* and *Manna Organics*.

Directions for the Assembly

Take two slices of bread. Spread Raw nut butter on one and spread Strawberry Chia Jam on another. Put them together and *enjoy your sammich!*

---

* If your strawberries are not sweet enough, you can add a little Raw agave nectar.

Zippy Energy Soup with Ginger Sweet Potato Fries

Yield 2 servings

Eating a great *Raw soup* served with something warm (cooked) and delicious is a great way to transition to Raw. So, here you go!

Zippy Energy Soup

⅔ cup water

⅓ cup fresh orange juice

2 cups kale

1 cup celery, chopped

1 cup romaine lettuce, chopped

1 cup red bell pepper, chopped

½ avocado, pitted and peeled

1 tablespoon Garlic Red Pepper Miso*

1 teaspoon fresh orange zest

¾–1 teaspoon wasabi powder (more or less as desired)

Blend everything together until creamy.

Ginger Sweet Potato Fries

1 large sweet potato

canola or olive oil

1–2 teaspoons ginger, freshly grated (or more!)

Himalayan crystal salt

black pepper

yacon syrup (optional, but worth it!)

Preheat the oven to 375 degrees F. Wash, peel, and cut the sweet potato into thick, julienne-like slices. Try to keep them similar in size so they cook evenly. Place the fries on a baking sheet. Drizzle them with a little canola oil. Sprinkle them with a little salt and pepper, and scatter the ginger on top.

Bake for 10–12 minutes. Turn the fries over and continue baking another 10–15 minutes (or until crispy on the outside and fork tender). Transfer the fries to a plate and drizzle a little yacon syrup on top.

* See Appendix B.

Veggie Burger Delight

Yield 2 servings

Veggie burgers that you buy in the store are a great transition food when you skip the bread and add some Raw foods to the plate. Here is a great way to have them.

> 2 veggie burgers*
>
> 2 slices tomato
>
> 1 large avocado, pitted, peeled and sliced
>
> pinch Himalayan crystal salt
>
> pinch black pepper
>
> 2 large carrots, cut into carrot sticks

Prepare the veggie burgers according the manufacturer's instructions. Top each burger with a slice of tomato and some sliced avocado. Sprinkle the salt and pepper on top. Serve the carrot sticks alongside. You can also serve this with Ginger Sweet Potato Fries (see previous recipe).

For more delicious flavor, I love adding a side of Cheezy Hemp Nacho Sauce (see recipe, Ch. 4) for both the carrot sticks and the burger!

---

* I love the veggie burgers by the company *Organic Sunshine Burgers*, which I get in the freezer department of Whole Foods Market. Check out their website: SunshineBurger.com

Green Hummus

Yield 3 cups

This makes a great Raw Transition Meal when served with a plate of fresh organic raw veggies. Green Hummus is extra healthy because it contains many raw ingredients. The chickpeas are the only cooked component (use chickpeas you prepare yourself so you can avoid BPA-lined cans). Of course, if you don't have time to make your own hummus, you can always buy it.

1 cup dry chickpeas/garbanzo beans (this makes
   approximately 2 cups cooked)

4 cups water (for cooking)

1 cup zucchini, chopped

1 cup spinach, gently packed

¼ cup + 1 tablespoon raw tahini

¼ cup fresh lemon juice

3 tablespoons fresh basil leaves, chopped

1 tablespoon raw olive oil

1 tablespoon raw sesame oil*

1 teaspoon garlic, pressed

¾ teaspoon cumin

¾ teaspoon Himalayan crystal salt

pinch black pepper

Place the chickpeas in a bowl with 3 cups of water. Let them soak like this for 8–10 hours. Drain the water. Place the soaked chickpeas in a pot with the 4 cups of water for cooking. Bring to a boil, then simmer for 2–3 hours (until desired tenderness is achieved).

Transfer them to a food processor, fitted with the "S" blade. Add the remaining ingredients and puree. Serve with fresh organic raw vegetables and fruit.

---

* If you don't have raw sesame oil, you can substitute raw olive oil. See Appendix B for details.

Superfly Fresh Sandwich

The next time you're making a sandwich with cooked bread (pita bread works great), load it with veggies and a Raw dressing or spread to make it a great Raw Vegan Transition recipe.

Ideas for filling and flavoring your sandwich are endless, which makes it exciting and fun. Here are some ideas: sprouts, cucumber slices, shredded carrot, sliced tomatoes, Raw sun-dried olives, soaked sun-dried tomatoes, Himalayan crystal salt, black pepper, chopped kale, sliced apple, diced mango or pineapple, avocado, peeled orange slices, lemon or lime juice, capers, Daiya cheese (which isn't Raw), minced broccoli, sauerkraut, green onion, shredded beet, banana, hemp seeds, raisins, etc.

Then, for extra Raw pizzaz, drizzle some Raw vegan dressing on top (see Cayenne Tahini Dressing, below) or use a Raw vegan spread (see Creamy Zinger Garlic Spread, below).

Cayenne Tahini Dressing

Yield 1 cup

This recipe is from my book, *Kristen Suzanne's EASY Raw Salads & Dressings*, available at KristensRaw.com

I love this easy 5-ingredient dressing. It is simple, delicious, and creamy. Don't let the "cayenne" in the title discourage you, as you can adjust the amount to suit your taste. Besides, cayenne is healthy for you! It can increase your metabolism, help your circulatory system, and it is beneficial for your stomach and intestinal tract.

¼–½ cup water or raw olive oil

½ cup raw tahini

3 tablespoons fresh lemon juice or lime juice

¼–½ teaspoon cayenne pepper

¼–½ teaspoon Himalayan crystal salt

Blend all of the ingredients until smooth, adding more water as needed.

Creamy Zinger Garlic Spread

Yield 1 ½ cups

This recipe is from my book, *Kristen Suzanne's EASY Raw Sides & Snacks*, available at KristensRaw.com

NOTE: You can have another great Raw Vegan Transition "snack" using Creamy Zinger Garlic Spread. For example, the next time you want cheese and crackers, use this for the cheese and enjoy it with some store bought organic crackers. Then, when you're ready to transition to more Raw, use Raw crackers!

> 1 cup raw cashews, macadamia nuts, or pine nuts
>
> 1 large clove garlic
>
> 1 tablespoon Garlic Red Pepper Miso*
>
> 1 tablespoon light miso
>
> 1 tablespoon fresh lemon juice
>
> 1 tablespoon extra virgin coconut oil
>
> a little water, if needed to help blend

Place the nuts in a bowl and cover with water plus about an inch. Let them soak for 1 hour. Drain off the water and give them a quick rinse. When the nuts are ready, blend all of the ingredients until creamy in your blender (or food processor).

* See Appendix B.

Superfood Sundae!

Ready for some kid-n-family friendly fun with food? The next time you scoop out vegan ice cream that you bought from the store, add the following Raw superfood toppings. And, don't forget to take a picture of them licking their bowls!

In addition to the Raw recipes below, you can use the following Raw goodies to make fun sundaes... chopped banana (or other fruit), raw nuts and seeds (almonds, pecans, walnuts, hemp seeds, chia seeds), raw cacao nibs, goji berries, mulberries, goldenberries, shredded (unsweetened) coconut.

THEN! The next step is making your own Raw ice cream so that the whole awesome dessert is Raw and full of wholesome good stuff. I've included a Raw vegan ice cream recipe below for when you're ready to take that step.

Awesome Raw Chocolate Sauce

Yield ¼ cup

¼ cup raw agave nectar or yacon syrup*
3 tablespoons raw chocolate powder (or raw carob powder)
pinch Himalayan crystal salt

Stir all of the ingredients together and drizzle on top of your ice cream. You can also add this to vegan milk so you can make chocolate milk.

* Using Raw agave nectar in this recipe really gives you a delicious chocolate experience. On the other hand, the yacon syrup (see NavitasNaturals.com) gives a unique flavor that is not completely chocolatey in my opinion, but still good. Some people might opt for yacon syrup because of its nutrient profile (see Appendix A for details on agave nectar and yacon syrup).

Sweet Strawberry Coulis

Yield 1 ½ cups

This is delicious with strawberries, but you can make it with any frozen fruit. Some of my other favorites are cherries, raspberries, blueberries, peaches, and blackberries.

1 (10 oz) bag frozen strawberries, thawed

¼ cup raw agave nectar

Blend the ingredients until smooth. Store any extra coulis in your refrigerator for up to five days. It's a great addition to any smoothie, too!

Maple Ice Cream

Yield approximately 2 ¾–3 cups

Raw ice cream rocks. Once you see how easy and fun it is to make it yourself, I bet you won't buy ice cream from the store again.

- ¾ cup raw cashews
- ¼ cup hemp seeds
- ¾ cup young Thai coconut water
- 1 cup young Thai coconut meat
- ½ cup raw agave nectar
- 1 tablespoon maple extract
- 2 teaspoons vanilla extract
- pinch Himalayan crystal salt
- 1 tablespoon psyllium husk powder

Grind the cashews to a fine grind using a blender or food processor fitted with the "S" blade. Place the ground cashews in a blender, add the remaining ingredients, except for the psyllium, and blend until creamy. Add the psyllium and blend to mix. Pour into a glass dish and freeze (a glass baking dish works well).

4
• • •

Raw Recipes to Make You Dance!

> So irresistible is the transformative power of enlightenment that your life seems to be shifted into a new dimension, opened to new and unsuspected possibilities.
>
> EUGEN HERRIGEL

This chapter is filled with scrumptious All-Raw recipes. Let me be more specific... these All-Raw recipes are going to make you want to dance all day long because they are delicious, fun, awesome, and filled with nutrition.

I included these Raw recipes for those of you who want to:

- Try some All-Raw recipes to experience what they're like and how they differ from Transitional Raw
- Graduate from the Transitional Raw stage to a level that regularly includes more All-Raw food in your life.
- "Wow" your family and friends with wonderful, unique, and delicious Raw recipes.

Get ready... you are about to load your body with mega delicious nutrition that tastes amazing and is going to make you so happy!

BEVERAGES

Fresh green juices and smoothies are great for transitioning to a Raw lifestyle. They are so healthy, that just the act of making and consuming them immediately makes you feel like you are taking a huge step toward lifelong, vibrant health.

Green juices are packed with powerful nutrients. They are alkalizing and can help curb cravings for caffeine and sugar. They're energizing, uplifting, and a great way to start the day.

I like my green juices extra smooth. Therefore, after I juice the ingredients, I like to strain the juice using a nut milk bag (or a paint strainer bag from a hardware store—much cheaper). To learn about my three favorite juicers and learn which might be best for your needs, visit my blog to see a video where I compare them:

http://kristensraw.blogspot.com/2009/11/new-juicer-comparison-video-green-star.html

I also love smoothies. These are great because they're filling, which can mean that you end up eating fewer cooked foods. I have a big smoothie for an entire meal sometimes. They fill you up with nutrients, fiber, and water, meaning they can be a great way to lose or manage your weight without feeling hungry. With smoothies, you can add vegan protein powders (and all kinds of powerful superfoods). Plus, they are incredibly fast and easy to make.

You'll see in these recipes that I like adding hemp seeds and hemp protein powder to my smoothies, especially when pregnant, breastfeeding, or when I'm working out a lot. Hemp is commonly referred to as a "superfood" because of its amazing nutritional value. Its amino acid profile dominates with the right balance of the 8 essential amino acids (10 if you're elderly or a baby), making it a vegetarian source of "complete" protein!

Chocolate Spice Hemp Shake

Yield 3 cups

Raw chocolate is one of my favorite ingredients and I love spicing it up with cinnamon and cayenne (a very popular combination). This recipe pleases my palate every time.

- 1 cup water
- 1 cup ice
- 2 medium bananas, peeled
- ¼ cup hemp protein powder
- 2 tablespoons hemp seeds
- 2 tablespoons raw chocolate powder
- ¼ teaspoon cinnamon
- ⅛ teaspoon cayenne (or more)

Blend everything together until creamy.

Frozen Banana Protein Shake

Yield 3 cups

The first time I made this, I loved it so much that I made it *seven times* in one week. I even snuck it into the movie one night, *packed in ice* (call me elaborate, but I like to bring my own healthy food to the movies since I won't go near the concession stand with a 10-foot pole!). I gave my husband a sip and he kept drinking it and drinking it (chugging is more like it)... until he got a brain freeze... that's when he finally gave it back.

> **1 cup water**
> **3 frozen bananas, chopped**
> **¼ cup hemp protein powder**
> **2 tablespoons hemp seeds**
> **1 tablespoon raw carob**

Blend everything until smooth and enjoy your frosty treat.

Variations:

- Replace the raw carob with raw chocolate powder.
- Add 2 tablespoons of raw almond butter (or any raw nut butter) to make it even richer. Add cinnamon, nutmeg, or pumpkin spice for extra flare.
- If you don't have frozen bananas, use ice and fresh bananas.

Creamy Raspberry Smoothie

Yield 1 quart

All I can say is YUM! This wonderful smoothie has a lot of fiber in it from the nutritious avocado and hemp protein powder. Digestive health, *here we come!*

> **2 cups water**
>
> **3 cups frozen raspberries (thawed a bit)**
>
> **½ avocado, pitted and peeled**
>
> **¼ cup (heaping) hemp protein powder**
>
> **dash vanilla extract**
>
> **drizzle raw agave nectar (to taste)**

Use a blender to blend everything until deliciously creamy.

Enchanted Island Hopping

Yield 2 ½ cups

This is a gorgeous light yellow smoothie filled with enchantment. You will really feel like you are on vacation when you're drinking it. This smoothie will put a smile on your face with the very first sip. So, if you find yourself stressed or overwhelmed... MAKE THIS! You'll be relaxed and smiling in no time.

> 1 cup water
>
> 2 cups pineapple, peeled and chopped
>
> 1 banana, peeled and chopped
>
> 1 tablespoon raw cashew butter
>
> 1 tablespoon coconut spread or coconut butter*

Blend all of the ingredients until smooth.

*See Appendix B.

Cherry Chocolate Bomb Shake!

Yield 2–3 cups

OH BOY! Are you ready? Here is one of my favorite concoctions! (And, it's not just one of *my* favorites. This recipe has made the Internet rounds because people are crazy about it.) I love it so much that, when I'm going to bed at night, I'm already looking forward to the next day when I get to make it. It's that good! I named it "Cherry Chocolate Bomb Shake!" because... frankly, it's the bomb! This fun shake is loaded with superior nutrition including superfood hemp seeds, Raw chocolate powder, and hemp protein powder, along with organic fruit.

Check out my video where I demonstrate how to make this unbelievable shake:

> http://kristensraw.blogspot.com/2010/02/raw-vegan-recipe-video-cherry-chocolate.html

1 cup water
1 frozen banana, chopped
1 cup frozen cherries
¼ cup hemp protein powder
2 tablespoons hemp seeds
2 tablespoons raw chocolate powder
splash vanilla extract

Blend this goodness and enjoy it as it helps make your day one of the best days ever!

Pregnant Momma Protein Shake

Yield 3–4 cups

During my pregnancy, I made this shake a lot. This recipe is loaded with nutrition including protein, essential fatty acids, fiber, and nutrients up the wazoo! Plus, I like that the vitamin C in the orange helps my body assimilate the iron in the spinach.

1 ½ cups water

2 cups spinach

2 bananas, peeled and chopped

1 orange, peeled and chopped

2 heaping tablespoons hemp protein powder

2 tablespoons hemp seeds

¼ teaspoon cinnamon

dash dulse flakes (or more!)

Blend it all up in your blender.

Ginger Cinnamon Fruit Smoothie

Yield 3 ½–4 cups

I started making variations of this recipe once when I was sick with bronchitis. A reader of my blog alerted me to the information that the ingredients black pepper, turmeric, and cinnamon can be helpful with bronchial health.

1–1 ½ cups water

1 ½ cups frozen blackberries, raspberries, or cherries

1 cup fresh pineapple

1 banana (frozen or fresh)

1 serving raw protein powder*

2 tablespoons hemp seeds

½–1 inch knob of fresh ginger

¼ teaspoon black pepper (or more)

½–1 teaspoon turmeric

½–1 teaspoon cinnamon

Blend it all up in your blender until smooth and creamy.

* I usually use Sun Warrior's Natural (plain) flavored sprouted brown rice protein.

Yummy Tummy Green Smoothie

Yield 2 ½–3 cups

When grapes are in season I love using them in my green smoothies. They add a delicious sweetness. The grapes combined with the orange and strawberries is like having a fruit basket in a cup. Fun!

1 cup water

15 grapes

1 orange, peeled and chopped

5 strawberries

2 handfuls spinach

pinch stevia (optional)

Give these fabulous ingredients a whirl in your blender. Drink it, feel your cells dancing with joy, and experience your tummy begging for more.

Garden Green Juice

Yield 3–4 cups

Fresh green juice is a staple in our family. We drink it many times a week. I can't imagine life without it because it is alkalizing, cleansing, nutritious, energizing, uplifting, delicious, and powerful.

> **2 large tomatoes**
> **⅓ bunch celery**
> **2 large cucumbers**
> **1 small bunch Swiss chard**

Juice all of the ingredients, adding a little water if desired.

Cucumber Wheat Grass Refresher

Yield 3 cups

Awesome. Delightful. Super nutritious. 'Nuff said!

2 large cucumbers

2 small apples

½ lemon

¼–½ cup water

1 tablespoon wheat grass powder*

Juice the cucumbers, apples, and lemon and transfer to a glass. Add the water. Stir in the wheat grass powder.

*See Appendix B.

Tangerine Love Green Juice

Yield 3–4 cups

Cucumbers and tangerines are a delicious combination. Add the celery and kale to the recipe, and you're getting superior nutrition with this recipe.

  2 large cucumbers

  4 tangerines, peeled

  ⅓ bunch celery

  1 bunch kale

Juice all of the ingredients.

Big-N-Fresh-N-Detox Juice

Yield 5 cups

Cilantro is hailed for its detoxifying capabilities, while the cucumbers and tomatoes make this recipe extra fresh tasting. And, the garlic? Well, not only does it add wonderful flavor, but it packs a nutritional punch!

> **2 large cucumbers**
> **1 bunch celery**
> **½ bunch kale**
> **½ bunch cilantro**
> **2 Roma tomatoes**
> **2 medium–large cloves garlic**

Juice all of the ingredients.

Cukes on Ice

Yield 1 serving

This recipe is so simple, but in all of the years I have been Raw and drinking cucumber juice, I've never enjoyed it more than this elegantly simple "recipe." It's supremely refreshing. Sure, you can add some mint, or a little cilantro or lime juice... those would all be delicious variations. But I'm quite fond of enjoying the cucumber juice (plain) and on ice. It's perfect for a hot summer day.

2–3 cucumbers

1 cup ice

Juice the cucumbers and pour over ice. Sit back, drink it, and chill out.

Kiwi Vitamin C

Kiwi is a powerhouse of nutrients. It is loaded with an army of disease-fighting phytonutrients, tons of vitamin C (twice as much as oranges!), magnesium, and potassium.

3 kiwi, peeled

5 celery stalks

8 romaine lettuce leaves

Juice all of the ingredients.

Spicy Plant Blood

Spice up your life with this recipe. It's fresh, exhilarating, and nutritious.

> **2 cucumbers**
>
> **1 head romaine lettuce**
>
> **1 red bell pepper**
>
> **⅓ bunch celery**
>
> **¼ lemon**
>
> **pinch cayenne pepper (or more!)**

Juice all of the ingredients except the cayenne. Stir in the cayenne pepper.

Brown Smoothie

Yield 4–5 cups

This particular smoothie is brown in color (not the sexiest), but it's fabulous in flavor and nutrition. The high level of vitamin C in the bell pepper helps the body assimilate the iron in the spinach.

> **1–2 cups water**
>
> **3 bananas, peeled**
>
> **1 red bell pepper, seeded and chopped**
>
> **1–2 handfuls of spinach**
>
> **hefty knob of ginger**

Blend all of the ingredients.

60-Second Raw Ranch Dressing (or Dip)

Yield 1 ½ cups

This dressing is named as such because it is quick and easy to make (okay, so maybe it takes some people two minutes to whip it up instead of 1 minute, but you get the point—it's really fast!). And, more important, it is plate-lickin' awesome. For real!

¾ **cup water**

½ **cup raw cashew butter**

1 tablespoon dried dill

1 tablespoon fresh lemon juice

1 teaspoon onion powder

½ **teaspoon Himalayan crystal salt**

pinch black pepper

Blend everything together until smooth.

This dressing thickens once it cools in the refrigerator for a while. At that point, you can use it as a luscious, flavorful thicker dip for dipping your veggies into.

But you can also still use it as salad dressing; by the time you put some on and toss the salad, the dressing thins out a bit. Or, you can put some in a little bowl, add some water, stir, and then pour it to dress your salad. This diluted variation will stretch it further and reduces the fat a bit (unless you eat all of it!).

Tart Goldenberry Dressing

Yield 1 cup

Goldenberries are one of my favorite treats. The first time I tasted them I squealed, *"Move over unhealthy, junky sour patch kids! I've got something so much better AND mega nutritious!"*

¼ cup goldenberries

⅓ cup fresh orange juice

2 tablespoons water

1 teaspoon yacon syrup (or raw agave nectar)

¼ teaspoon vanilla extract

¼ teaspoon Himalayan crystal salt

pinch black pepper, or more

¼ cup raw olive oil

Place the goldenberries in a bowl and add enough water to cover them. Let them soak for up to an hour. Drain the water off. Once the goldenberries are ready, blend all of the ingredients, except for the olive oil, until quite smooth. It might take a little longer to blend the goldenberries well. Then, while the blender is on low speed, drizzle the olive oil into the blender.

Ginger Shallot Dressing

Yield 1 cup

This is one of my favorite dressings. It has a gorgeous flavor and it's easy to make.

- 5 tablespoons raw olive oil
- 3 tablespoons apple cider vinegar
- 2 tablespoons water
- 2 tablespoons raw agave nectar
- 1 tablespoon + ½ teaspoon tamari, wheat-free
- 1 tablespoon shallot, minced (or 1 teaspoon onion powder)
- 1 tablespoon fresh ginger, grated (or 1 teaspoon ginger powder)
- ⅛ teaspoon black pepper

Blend all of the ingredients together using a blender.

Pineapple Orange Kale Salad

Yield 2 servings

I never go very long without including fresh organic raw kale in my diet. Kale is a potent leafy green that's full of nutrients for helping to fight cancer and keep you healthy.

- 1 large bunch dinosaur kale
- 2 tablespoons fresh lemon juice
- 1 medium clove garlic, pressed
- ½ teaspoon Himalayan crystal salt
- dash black pepper
- dash nutmeg
- 1 avocado, pitted, peeled, and diced
- 1 orange, peeled, segmented, and diced
- ½ cup pineapple, diced

Remove the stems from the kale. You can leave the more tender parts of the stem (toward the top of each leaf) in the salad, but the harder stems toward the bottom of each leaf should be removed. Tear apart the kale leaves (or use a knife and chop them) into bite-size pieces.

Place the torn (or chopped) kale into a large bowl. Add the lemon juice, garlic, salt, pepper, nutmeg, and avocado. Massage all of these ingredients together with your hands (squishing the avocado into the kale) for a good 30–60 seconds. Add the orange and pineapple, and gently toss to mix.

Dilly Orange Coleslaw

Yield approximately 2 quarts

My husband is not a huge fan of traditional coleslaw. But when he ate his first serving of this, he literally told me *four* times, "Kristen, this is really good. Like, I mean *really* good. You said we were having coleslaw and I was cool with that, but *I didn't expect this!*"

For the Salad

3 cups purple cabbage, shredded

2 cups carrots, shredded

2 cups zucchini, shredded

2 cups orange, peeled, segmented, and diced

½ cup dried mulberries (or golden raisins)

For the Dressing

1 cup water

½ cup + 2 tablespoons raw cashew butter

3 tablespoons fresh lime or lemon juice

2–3 tablespoons dried wakame flakes*

1 tablespoon dried dill

2 teaspoons ginger powder

½ teaspoon Himalayan crystal salt

¼ teaspoon black pepper

Place the salad components in a large bowl and set aside. Use a blender and blend the dressing ingredients. Pour the blended dressing mixture over the salad components and stir until all of the salad is covered with dressing.

Serving suggestion:

- To add some protein and make this a Raw Vegan Transition recipe, follow the cooking instructions for tofu in the Spinach Ranch Tofu Salad recipe (see recipe, Ch. 2) and add some on top when you serve Dilly Orange Coleslaw.

*See Appendix B.

Thrive Salad

I absolutely love Thrive Salad. It has fresh, vibrant, "wake-you-up" flavors! My favorite time of day to enjoy this? Morning! It's an awesome way to start the day.

> 1 grapefruit, peeled, seeded, and chopped
>
> 2 kiwi, peeled and diced
>
> 1 apple, cored and chopped
>
> ½ avocado, pitted and peeled
>
> drizzle raw agave nectar

Place everything in a bowl and feel your body thrive with each and every bite.

Must-Make Kale Salad

Yield 2 servings

½ cup sun-dried tomatoes

1 large bunch curly kale

2–2 ½ tablespoons fresh lemon juice

2–2 ½ tablespoons raw olive oil

½ teaspoon Himalayan crystal salt

dash black pepper

1 red bell pepper, seeded and diced

1 orange, peeled, seeded, and chopped

5 raw olives, pitted and chopped

3 tablespoons raisins

Place the sun-dried tomatoes in a bowl and add enough water to cover them. Let them soak for up to an hour. Drain the water off and chop them.

Remove the stems from the kale. You can leave the more tender parts of the stem (toward the top of each leaf) in the salad, but the harder stems toward the bottom of each leaf should be removed. Tear apart the kale leaves (or use a knife and chop them) into bite-size pieces. Place the torn kale into a large bowl. Add the lemon juice, olive oil, salt, and pepper. Massage all of these ingredients together with your hands for 30-60 seconds. Add the remaining ingredients and gently toss to mix.

Garden Guacamole

Yield approximately 4–5 cups

One of the awesome things about this recipe is that I consider it "guacamole lite," meaning it's lower in fat than traditional guacamole. Personally, it's hard for me to stop eating guacamole once I start, and it's not long before I've consumed a lot of fat as a result. Therefore, I lowered this recipe's fat content per serving by filling it up with fat-free, non-sweet fruits and vegetables. Note that a lot of people easily lose weight on a Raw vegan diet even if they consume plenty of Raw vegan fats (from nuts, seeds, avocados, etc.). However, some people attempting to lose weight hit a plateau and wonder what to do next. For cases like that, I usually recommend cutting back on fat and that's usually all it takes.

 3 avocados, pitted, peeled and diced

 juice from 2 limes

 ½–¾ teaspoon Himalayan crystal salt

 1 tomato, diced

 1 red bell pepper, seeded and diced

 1 orange bell pepper, seeded and diced

 3 stalks celery, diced

 ½ bunch cilantro leaves, chopped

Place the diced avocado into a large bowl with the lime juice and salt. Smash it up (I like using a potato masher to do the job). Add the remaining ingredients and stir to mix. At this point, taste it and see if you'd like to add more salt.

Variations:

- I enjoy mine scooped onto organic red leaf or romaine lettuce that I use as a wrap, like a burrito. My husband loves his on whole grain, organic toast.

- For this recipe, I used medium-size, non-sweet fruits, but you could use large. You could substitute the tomato with cucumber or add diced zucchini... there are all kinds of options. Shredded carrots would be delish, too. Mango would be heavenly! Try different options and keep it colorful. That's half the fun of it!

Creamy Rosemary Avocado Dressing

Yield 1 cup

This is a thick and creamy dressing, yet the flavor and experience come across as on the lighter side. I attribute this to the "fluffiness" of blended avocado and the freshness of the rosemary. (Truth be told, I've eaten a whole batch of this "dressing" recipe... *as a soup!*)

This recipe also includes wakame, which is a sea vegetable. I personally am not a fan of sea veggies due to their flavor, but their nutrient profile is so impressive that I make it a point to get them into my diet. I usually just try to hide their flavor with other ingredients.

> ½ cup fresh orange juice
>
> ¼ cup water, more if desired
>
> 1 avocado, pitted and peeled
>
> 2 teaspoons fresh rosemary
>
> 2 teaspoons wakame flakes (or more)
>
> ½ teaspoon Himalayan crystal salt
>
> ⅛ teaspoon black pepper

Blend everything together until smooth. This dressing is best used right away.

Mushroom Vegetable Harvest Soup

See photo at KristensRaw.com/photos.

Yield 3 ½ cups

If you enjoy the taste of fresh mushrooms, then you definitely want to try this delightful soup recipe. It is full of nutrition and makes a wonderful starter to any lunch or dinner.

> 1 cup fresh carrot juice
>
> 2 cups zucchini, chopped and packed
>
> 2 cups portabella mushrooms, chopped and packed
>
> 1 stalk celery, chopped
>
> 3 tablespoons fresh orange juice
>
> 2 tablespoons raw olive oil
>
> 1 tablespoon light miso
>
> 2 teaspoons onion powder
>
> dash cayenne pepper (optional)
>
> dash black pepper

Blend everything together until smooth. If you'd like the soup a tad warm, just blend it a little longer.

Kick-Ass Raw Soup

Yield 4 ½ cups

Yup, I swore in the title. But, I found that I really had no choice. This soup is P-A-C-K-E-D with nutrition, and it's so tasty... and *that is* why it's so kick ass!

 ½ cup water

 ⅓ cup hemp seeds

 2 cups kale, destemmed and packed

 1 ½ cups apple, cored and chopped

 1 ½ cups cucumber, chopped

 1 cup celery, chopped

 1 cup red (or orange) bell pepper, chopped

 1 cup tomato, chopped

 2 tablespoons wakame flakes

 1 tablespoon raw sunflower lecithin*

 1 teaspoon onion powder

 ½ teaspoon Himalayan crystal salt

 ⅛ teaspoon black pepper

Blend everything until smooth-ish (I say "ish" because leaving a little bit of texture can be nice).

*See KristensRaw.com/store for details.

Soft Soup

Weird name for a soup, right? It fits though. This soup is soft in texture and flavor, and... it will keep you coming back for more. Make it and you'll see what I mean!

1 cup fresh cucumber juice

1 cup young Thai coconut water

¾ cup young Thai coconut meat

¾ cup avocado, pitted, peeled, and chopped

¼ teaspoon Himalayan crystal salt (more to taste)

dash black pepper

Blend everything until creamy. Serve immediately.

Kristen's Cacao Cookie Crumble

Yield approximately 10 servings

There are many ways to enjoy this delectable treat. My husband and I eat it plain, in a little cup. My mom loves it with a cup of organic decaf coffee. We also like to slice organic bananas and sprinkle it on top. Adding it on top of Raw vegan ice cream or mousse is superb. It's versatile, as many Raw vegan foods are, so it can be enjoyed as part of a breakfast, lunch, dessert, or snack.

    1 cup raw almonds

    1 cup raw cashews

    1 vanilla bean

    ½ cup raw chocolate powder

    1 teaspoon chocolate extract

    pinch Himalayan crystal salt

    14 medjool dates, pitted and chopped

Using a food processor, fitted with the "S" blade, process the nuts until they are a coarse grind. Slice the vanilla bean lengthwise and scrape the insides out with a spoon or knife. Add it to the food processor along with the chocolate powder, chocolate extract, and salt, and pulse briefly to mix. Add the chopped dates and process until thoroughly combined like a chunky crumble. *Note:* The longer you process this, the more oils get released from the nuts making it stick together more.

Goji Wonder Treats

Yield 20–25 treats

I love goji berries and I love creating recipes which feature them. They have so much nutrition that they make a regular appearance in my family's diet. In fact, I keep a little cup of goji berries mixed with raisins on our kitchen counter next to a bowl of hemp seeds for fast, superfood snacking.

> 1 cup raw almonds
>
> 1 cup goji berries
>
> 1 cup dried coconut, shredded and unsweetened
>
> ¾ cup soft dates, pitted and gently packed
>
> ¼ cup raw cacao butter, liquid
>
> 3 tablespoons raw agave nectar
>
> pinch Himalayan crystal salt

Grind the almonds in a food processor, fitted with the "S" blade, until they're a coarse grind. Add the remaining ingredients and process until the mixture begins to stick together enough that you can form raw cookies with it. Using a heaping tablespoon as your measurement, portion the batter and form the cookies into desired shapes.

Sunny Lemon Macaroons

Yield 33–34 macaroons

I sent these with my husband to work one day to share with his clients and one of them sat there smelling it for a good 2–3 minutes before she even took a bite. Everyone loved them!

1 cup raw almonds

1 cup dried coconut, shredded and unsweetened

⅔ cup coconut butter*

½ cup hemp seeds

½ cup raw agave nectar

4 medjool dates, pitted and diced

2 tablespoons fresh lemon zest

1 ¼ teaspoon lemon extract

pinch Himalayan crystal salt

Using a food processor, fitted with the "S" blade, grind the almonds to a course grind. Transfer to a bowl and add the remaining ingredients. Stir everything together, or mash it together with your hands. Or, make it easier and mix it all together using a mixer with a paddle-like attachment. Using a 1-tablespoon size ice cream scooper, portion out the macaroons. I like to store these in my freezer.

* See Appendix B.

Mesquite Protein Chocolate

Yield 12 chocolates

These are very rich and dense in dark chocolate flavor and nutrients (including protein from the chocolate, hemp and mesquite). One of the ways to help keep me satisfied in my Raw vegan lifestyle is having Raw chocolates on hand *at all times*, so I keep a variety of them in my freezer.

> 1 vanilla bean
>
> ⅔ cup raw cacao liquor, liquid*
>
> 3 tablespoons raw agave nectar
>
> 3 tablespoons hemp seeds
>
> 1 tablespoon mesquite powder
>
> ½ teaspoon vanilla extract

Slice the vanilla bean lengthwise and scrape the insides out with a spoon or knife. Stir all of the ingredients together in a small bowl. Portion out the Raw chocolates, using a 1-tablespoon measuring spoon, onto a plate lined with wax paper, or portion into mini-candy paper cups. Place in the freezer for 10–15 minutes or until firm. Store in your freezer until you're ready to serve them.

* See Appendix B.

Chocolate Coconut Duet

Yield 12–13 chocolates

Hhhmmm… one of my favorite flavor combos is chocolate and coconut. These really hit the spot, especially in the middle of the night. Trust me, you cannot go wrong with these.

> ⅓ cup raw cacao liquor, liquid*
>
> ¼ cup coconut spread or coconut butter, softened*
>
> ¼ cup dried coconut, shredded and unsweetened
>
> 2 tablespoons raw agave nectar
>
> 1 ½ teaspoons coconut extract

Stir all of the ingredients together in a small bowl. Portion out the Raw chocolates, using a 1-tablespoon measuring spoon, onto a plate lined with wax paper, or portion into mini-candy paper cups. Place in the freezer for 10–20 minutes.

* See Appendix B.

Treasure Chest Chocolate Bark

Yield 15–20 pieces

This recipe is great for two reasons: I love its consistency. It's filled with different textures from the dried berries, hemp seeds, etc... reminding me of a treasure chest filled with goodies. Then, I love the flavor and nutritional profile of each ingredient.

¾ cup raw cacao liquor, liquid

½ cup yacon syrup* (or ¼ cup raw agave nectar)

1 tablespoon raw sunflower lecithin (see Appendix B)

2 teaspoons vanilla extract

¼ cup goji berries

¼ cup dried mulberries

¼ cup hemp seeds

¼ cup raisins

Stir the cacao liquor, yacon (or agave), lecithin, and vanilla together in a bowl. Add the remaining ingredients and stir until combined. Spread the mixture onto a cookie sheet, fitted with a piece of wax paper. Place the tray in the freezer for 10–20 minutes. After it has hardened, take it off the tray, peel off the wax paper, and break into pieces.

* Yacon has a molasses-type flavor and it is not as sweet as raw agave nectar. If you prefer a sweeter chocolate, opt for raw agave nectar, or perhaps a mix of them both. For details about yacon syrup, see Appendix A.

Mocha Orange Chocolates

Yield 24–30 small chocolates

I've always loved the flavors chocolate, coffee, and orange, and when they are together—*simply amazing*. If you like these flavors, too, then you will love Mocha Orange Chocolates.

> ¾ cup raw cacao liquor, liquid
>
> ¼ cup + 1 tablespoon raw agave nectar
>
> 1 tablespoon Teeccino, ground*
>
> 1 teaspoon fresh orange zest, packed
>
> ½ teaspoon coffee extract
>
> ½ teaspoon orange extract

Stir all of the ingredients together in a small bowl. Fill small candy paper cups with the chocolate. One way to make this easy is to fill an empty squirt-style bottle with the chocolate mixture (like an empty raw agave nectar bottle). Then, you can easily squirt the chocolate mixture into the candy paper cups. Place in the freezer for 10–20 minutes. Enjoy!

* See Appendix B.

Ginger Spice Carrot Cake

See photo at KristensRaw.com/photos.

Yield 7 or 8-inch square springform pan (approximately 6–8 pieces)

Vanilla Ginger Frosting Ingredients

   ½ cup coconut spread or coconut butter (see Appendix B)

   ½ cup raw agave nectar (light or dark)

   2 teaspoons vanilla extract

   2 teaspoons fresh ginger, grated

Cake Ingredients

   1 cup raw pecans

   2 tablespoons flax meal

   1 tablespoon ginger powder

   1 teaspoon cinnamon

   ⅛ teaspoon nutmeg

   ⅓ cup dried coconut, shredded and unsweetened

   4 ounces dried yacon slices, ground (about 1 cup)*

   12 medjool dates, pitted and diced

   2 cups carrots, shredded and packed

   2 cups apples, shredded and packed

The Frosting Directions

Blend all of the ingredients together. Set aside in a bowl while you make the cake. If the frosting starts to solidify too much before pouring on the cake, warm it slightly in the dehydrator for a few minutes prior to frosting the cake. (If you don't have a dehydrator, you can set it on top of a toaster oven for a few minutes.)

The Cake Directions

Place the pecans, flax meal, ginger, cinnamon, and nutmeg in a food processor, fitted with the "S" blade, and process until the pecans reach a grind of slightly coarse. Transfer to a large bowl, add the dried coconut, and set aside.

In a separate bowl, put the ground yacon, dates, and carrots together. Before adding the apples to this bowl, squeeze out some of the juice (this helps reduce the wetness.) Add the apples to the bowl along with the carrots and toss together.

Add the carrot mixture to the pecan mixture and toss to mix. Next, put ⅓–½ of the cake mixture in the food processor, fitted with the "S" blade, and briefly process it so it breaks the components down a bit, but do not over process it. Transfer it to a bowl. Do this with the remainder of the cake mixture.

Press half of the batter, gently, but firmly, into a square or round springform pan. Follow that with the other half of the cake mixture on top, and gently, but firmly, press it down. (I like to do this in two steps to make sure it gets pressed evenly.)

Pour the frosting evenly on top. Place the cake in the refrigerator for up to an hour to solidify the frosting. If desired, you can drizzle a little yacon syrup on top before serving, as shown in the photo at KristensRaw.com/photos. (See Appendix B for information on yacon syrup.)

* Before grinding the yacon slices, place them in the freezer for 10–15 minutes to make them easier to grind. Then, using a food processor, fitted with the "S" blade, grind the yacon slices. You might want to do this in two batches. Dried yacon slices are available from NavitasNaturals.com, other online sources, as well as some health food stores.

Sweet Frosting/Dip

Yield ⅓ cup

This is a dangerously awesome recipe. You've been warned! My favorite way to enjoy it? You mean, other than straight off a spoon? I dip fruit into it (strawberries are heavenly) and my fingers as well! It is great drizzled on top of Raw cookies and brownies. And, of course, it can make a lovely frosting for your next Raw cake. You probably want to make more than one recipe's worth!

¼ **cup coconut spread or coconut butter (see Appendix B)**
¼ **cup raw agave nectar**
½ **teaspoon almond, vanilla, or orange extract (or other flavors)**

Combine all of the ingredients until smooth using a blender, or as I prefer, a mini-food processor, fitted with the "S" blade. This is ready to enjoy immediately. If you put it in the refrigerator, it will solidify into a thick frosting.

Chocolate Frosting/Dip

Yield ½ cup

Mmmm... much like the Sweet Frosting/Dip in the previous recipe, this delectable dessert can be devoured by the spoonful or you can get fancy and drizzle it on top of banana slices or berries. It can also be used as a frosting for Raw cakes, brownies, and cookies.

¼ cup coconut spread or coconut butter (see Appendix B)

¼ cup raw agave nectar

2 tablespoons raw chocolate powder

Combine all of the ingredients until smooth using a blender, or as I prefer, a mini-food processor, fitted with the "S" blade. This is ready to enjoy immediately. If you put it in the refrigerator, it will solidify into a thick frosting.

Candy Bites

Yield 12 candies

I love recipes that can be put together super fast. I love them even more when they're sweet like candy. And, I love them even more *when they're healthy!*

Candy Bites, with a tall, cold glass of plant-based milk, make a terrific after-school snack for kids. But, they're not just for kids! They make a great after-work snack for adults along with a nice warm cup of herbal tea or Teeccino™.

> 7 soft medjool dates, pitted
>
> 3 tablespoons coconut spread or coconut butter, softened (see Appendix B)
>
> 2 teaspoons raw carob (or raw chocolate powder)
>
> pinch Himalayan crystal salt

Using a food processor, fitted with the "S" blade, process all of the ingredients together until crumbly. Take a 1-tablespoon measuring spoon and scoop out a slightly heaping tablespoon, gently pack it, and then roll it into a ball in your hand. Repeat until all of the candy batter is used. Place the balls in the refrigerator. You'll notice they are a little oily and squishy when forming them into balls. Once you place them in the refrigerator they'll firm up.

Easy Pecan Cookies

Yield 2 cups cookie batter

Pecans are good for you. They have phytosterols, vitamin E, potassium, fiber, and more. And, let's not forget… they taste great!

> 1 ½ cups raw pecans
>
> pinch Himalayan crystal salt
>
> 1 tablespoon raw agave nectar
>
> 1 tablespoon coconut oil
>
> 8 medjool dates, pitted and chopped

Process the pecans and salt in a food processor, fitted with the "S" blade, until coarsely ground. Add the agave, coconut oil, and dates and process until thoroughly incorporated. Form into cookies of desired size.

Raw Fiesta Tacos

Yield approximately 6 tacos

The Components

5–8 romaine lettuce leaves

1–2 medium tomatoes, diced

¾–1 cup Cheezy Hemp Nacho Sauce (see recipe, Ch. 4)

For the Taco "Meat"

Yield approximately 2 cups

1 cup raw walnuts

1 cup portabella mushroom, chopped

½ cup hemp seeds

½ cup fresh cilantro

juice of ½ lime (use the whole lime if it's not really juicy)

2 teaspoons raw chocolate powder

1 teaspoon chili powder

1 teaspoon onion powder

1 teaspoon mesquite powder

½ teaspoon cumin

¼–½ teaspoon Himalayan crystal salt

Directions for the Taco "Meat"

Place the walnuts in a bowl and cover with water plus about an inch. Let them soak for 6–8 hours. Drain off the water and give them a quick rinse.

Once the walnuts are ready to use, process all of the ingredients using a food processor, fitted with the "S" blade, until it resembles the texture of ground meat.

Directions for the Assembly

Start with a leaf of romaine lettuce and spoon some taco meat down the middle. Then add some Cheezy Hemp Nacho Sauce (see recipe, Ch. 4) and top that with diced tomatoes. If you have leftover sauce, this is great as a dip for organic corn chips, raw vegetables, and as a dressing on salad.

Kristen Suzanne's Italian Lasagna #2

See photo at KristensRaw.com/photos.

Yield one square springform pan or glass baking dish
(approximately 7 × 7)

This recipe is involved but it is so amazing! Trust me: It's the bomb! Frankly, it is enough to convert any skeptic to the delights of Raw. This recipe is similar to the lasagna recipe in my book, *Kristen Suzanne's EASY Raw Vegan Entrees*, but I've changed things up a bit, hence, the "#2" in the title.

For the Noodles

1–2 medium zucchini, sliced into approximately $1/16$ inch thick rounds (about 40 slices, 1.5" in diameter)

Place the zucchini rounds on a mesh dehydrator tray and dehydrate at 125 degrees F for 25 minutes. If you do not have a dehydrator, then just set them aside in a single layer until you are ready to use them.

For the Marinara

1 cup sun-dried tomatoes

4 medium tomatoes, quartered

1 red, orange, or yellow bell pepper, seeded and chopped

2 green onions (green and white parts), chopped

7 sun-dried olives, pitted, and chopped* (or any olives)

⅓ cup fresh basil leaves, gently packed

½ cup fresh Italian (flat leaf) parsley, gently packed

2 tablespoons raw olive oil

1 tablespoon balsamic vinegar

1 teaspoon Italian seasoning

1 clove garlic, minced

¼ teaspoon Himalayan crystal salt

dash black pepper

Place the sun-dried tomatoes in a bowl and add enough water to cover them. Let them soak for up to an hour. Drain the water off.

Once the sun-dried tomatoes are soaked and ready to use, place all of the ingredients in a food processor, fitted with the "S" blade, and pulse the mixture until you reach a thick texture (keep it a little chunky so it doesn't get too wet). Place the marinara in a fine mesh strainer, over a bowl, to drain off excess water while you prepare the remaining components to the lasagna. You don't want marinara that is too wet or it will have trouble holding together in the lasagna. You can come back to the marinara every 5–10 minutes, while it is straining, and press on it with a rubber spatula to help force more draining. Reserve the strained marinara juice because you will use it when making the Ricotta Cheeze.

For the Mushrooms**

2 large portabella mushrooms, diced (approximately 3 ½ cups)

1 ½ tablespoons tamari, wheat-free

1 ½ tablespoons raw olive oil

2 teaspoons fresh lemon juice

pinch of black pepper

Toss the mushrooms in the tamari, oil, lemon juice, and pepper. Set aside for at least 10 minutes to marinate. Drain well and gently squeeze to remove excess liquid.

For the Ricotta Cheeze

2 cups raw Brazil nuts

1 clove garlic

2 teaspoons nutritional yeast (optional, this is not raw)

2 teaspoons tamari, wheat-free

dash nutmeg

pinch black pepper

5–6 tablespoons strained juice from the marinara

Using a food processor, fitted with the "S" blade, process all of the ingredients until it is a thick puree.

For the Spinach

1 (5 oz) bag spinach

Briefly chop the spinach in a food processor, fitted with the "S" blade, and set aside.

Directions for the Assembly

Spread a thin, sparse layer of the marinara on the bottom of a glass baking dish or springform pan (I prefer a springform with this recipe because it's easier to cut the lasagna out of this kind of pan). Place a layer of zucchini on top of the sparse layer of marinara (don't overlap the zucchinis). Spread another layer of the marinara over the zucchini, making it a little thicker this time.

Then, spread a layer of the mushroom mixture and press gently. Place a layer of the cheeze on top of that, followed by a layer of the spinach, and continue layering: zucchini, marinara, mushrooms, cheeze, and spinach. Press gently, but firmly, between each layer.

Keep layering until you get to the top of your pan or until you run out of lasagna components. It's easiest to do this process using a small offset spatula and your hands.

Serve immediately at room temperature or warmed slightly in the dehydrator at 135 degrees F for an hour (or at 105 degrees F for 1–2 hours). Store leftovers in an airtight container in the refrigerator for up to three days.

If you're using a springform pan, you might want to roll up some paper towel (4 pieces, one for each side) and stuff it around the outside of the pan. If any water seeps out, this will help absorb it.

Have leftover components that didn't get used in the lasagna? No problem! When this happens, I stir it all up in a bowl and eat it like goulash! It's delicious!

---

* To easily pit the olives, place them all on a clean surface and simply press down on them with a spatula. This will crack the skin and make the pits easy to extract.

** If you're not a fan of mushrooms, I still recommend trying this recipe as is. My husband doesn't like mushrooms but he loves this recipe. The mushrooms give it a heartier, meat-like texture rather than a lot of mushroom flavor.

Fresh Raw Zucchini & Cucumber Pasta

Yield 2 servings

1 cucumber, spiralized*

1 zucchini, spiralized

juice of 1 fresh lemon

1 red bell pepper, seeded and diced

1 avocado, pitted, peeled, and diced

corn cut from 1 fresh cob

Toss all of the ingredients together in a bowl and serve.

Variations:

- Instead of avocado, use Raw olive oil and lemon juice.
- Add chopped olives and soaked sun-dried tomatoes.
- Replace the red bell pepper with shredded carrot and add fresh herbs such as cilantro, basil, and/or parsley.
- Sprinkle hemp seeds on top for more protein and essential fatty acids.
- Make it spicy by adding minced red Serrano pepper or jalapeno pepper.

* I use a *Benriner Turning Slicer* to make my Raw vegan pasta, available at KristensRaw .com/store. Or you can make fettuccini-style (flat, ribbon-like) noodles by using a vegetable peeler.

Garlic Mustard Kelp Noodles

Yield 2 servings

In all of the years that I have been Raw, I've avoided most sea veggies directly (I hide dulse, kelp, and wakame in some recipes, but that's usually where I draw the line). Therefore, kelp noodles were something I didn't have in my diet. I was not crazy about either their taste or texture. But I recently accidentally ordered some in a Raw restaurant (not actually realizing that I ordered kelp noodles), and I was blown away by how much I enjoyed them. I decided that I must come up with a simple and delicious recipe to eat them at home. For me, the trick to liking these sea veggies involves two steps: 1) thoroughly rinsing and soaking the noodles to rid them of their sea flavor and to soften them a bit, and 2) using a creamy, strong flavored sauce, like the one below.

1 (12 oz) package kelp noodles*

juice of 1 lime

⅓ cup raw cashews

3 tablespoons Raw Mustard (see next recipe)

2 tablespoons hemp seeds

1 medium-large clove garlic

1 teaspoon fresh orange zest

pinch Himalayan crystal salt

6 tablespoons water

1 orange, peeled, seeded, and chopped

Rinse the kelp noodles well and place them in a bowl. Add the lime juice. Add water until the noodles are just barely covered with the water/lime juice mix. Let them soak for an hour. Drain the kelp noodles and give them a quick rinse. Place them in a bowl by themselves and set aside.

Place the cashews in a bowl and cover with water plus about an inch. Let them soak for 1 hour. Drain off the water and give them a quick rinse. Blend the cashews, mustard, hemp seeds, garlic, orange zest, salt, and 6 tablespoons of water. It doesn't have to be really creamy. In fact, I rather prefer the little grit-size cashew pieces, because it adds the perfect texture to the dish. Pour the sauce over the noodles and toss until all of the noodles are coated. Divide and serve in two bowls. Top each bowl with ½ of the chopped orange.

* I buy kelp noodles at Whole Foods Market, but they are also available online.

Raw Mustard

Yield approximately 1 cup

2 teaspoons yellow mustard seeds, soaked 1–2 hours, then drained

½ cup extra virgin olive oil or hemp oil

1 tablespoon dry mustard powder

1 tablespoon apple cider vinegar

1 tablespoon fresh lemon juice or lime juice

¼ cup raw agave nectar

½ teaspoon Himalayan crystal salt

¼ teaspoon turmeric

Blend all of the ingredients together until smooth. It might be very thick, so if you want, add some water or oil to thin it out. If it's too spicy for your taste, adding more oil will help reduce the "heat."

Variation:

- "Honey" Mustard Version: Add more Raw agave nectar (until you reach the desired sweetness).

Paradise Mango & Pâté Wrap

See photo at KristensRaw.com/photos.

Yield 2 wraps

This meal comes wrapped in large leafy greens to hold everything together. Using greens in place of bread is hardcore!

- 2 large collard greens
- 2 carrots, shredded
- 1 mango, peeled, pitted, and sliced
- 1 cup Nutrient Sunflower Pâté (see recipe, below)

Nutrient Sunflower Pâté

Yield approximately 2 ½ cups

- ¾ cup raw sunflower seeds
- ½ cup sun-dried tomatoes
- 1 ½ cups red bell pepper, chopped
- 1 cup celery, chopped
- 4 raw olives, pitted and minced
- 1 tablespoon jalapeno pepper, minced
- 1 tablespoon fresh grapefruit juice
- 1 tablespoon chia seeds
- 2 teaspoons nutritional yeast (optional, this is not raw)
- 1 teaspoon mustard seed powder
- ½ teaspoon dulse flakes

½ teaspoon poultry seasoning

¼ teaspoon Herbamere™

Place the sunflower seeds in a bowl and cover with water plus about an inch. Let them soak for 6–8 hours. Drain off the water and give them a quick rinse. Place the sun-dried tomatoes in another bowl and add enough water to cover them. Let them soak for up to an hour. Drain the water off into another bowl and keep it for use later in the recipe, if needed. Once the sunflower seeds and sun-dried tomatoes are ready, use a food processor, fitted with the "S" blade, to process all of the ingredients until thoroughly mixed. You can moisten it more by adding some of the reserved sun-dried tomato soak water, if desired.

Take a collard leaf and cut out the bottom part of the stem. Spread pâté on the leaf and add some shredded carrots and sliced mango. Roll up and eat. Use toothpicks to hold it together if desired. Store any leftover pâté in an airtight container in the refrigerator for up to five days—this can be enjoyed with chopped veggies or on top of salads.

Creamy Raw Vegan Yogurt

Yield approximately 1 cup

Probiotics are live microorganisms that are good for you, such as those that live in your gut and aid with digestion. To make a Raw vegan (non-dairy) yogurt, we add probiotic powder.

1 cup young Thai coconut meat, packed

¼ cup young Thai coconut water

⅛ teaspoon Ejuva's Moflora probiotic powder*

Blend the coconut meat and water together until smooth. Add the probiotic powder and briefly blend it. Pour the coconut mixture into a glass mason jar and put the lid on it. Let this set on your countertop for 12–24 hours, depending on the level of tartness desired (the longer it sits, the more tart it will become).

Variations:

- Enjoy plain or sweetened with Raw agave nectar or minced dates. Add fruits (stir in as bite size pieces or blend in before serving): berries, pineapple, banana, papaya, etc. Add hemp seeds, cacao nibs, goji berries or other superfoods.

*Available at Ejuva.com. Or, you can empty the contents of a capsule of whatever probiotic you have on hand.

Garlic Olive Spread

Yield 1 cup

I was pregnant when I came up with this recipe. I was sitting at the computer craving salty olives, creamy cashews, and zesty garlic. What did I come up with? A delicious spread that is perfect for any of the following: spreading on cooked veggie burgers, dipping fresh veggies into, slathering on a Raw wrap sandwich, or just licking off your fingers.

> ⅔ cup raw cashews
>
> 10 raw olives*
>
> 3 tablespoons raw olive oil
>
> 2 teaspoons fresh lime juice
>
> 1 teaspoon garlic, pressed
>
> ½ teaspoon onion powder
>
> ⅛ teaspoon Himalayan crystal salt (optional)
>
> pinch black pepper
>
> 2–3 tablespoons water, if needed

Place the cashews in a bowl and cover with water plus about an inch. Let them soak for 30–60 minutes. Drain off the water and give them a quick rinse.

Blend everything together until smooth and creamy.

* For this recipe, I love using *Essential Living Foods' Black Bojita Olives* available at Whole Foods Markets or online at EssentialLivingFoods.com.

Hearty Buckwheat Biscuits

See photo at KristensRaw.com/photos.

Yield 6–10 biscuits (I usually cut mine big, so I get about 6 in a batch)

These biscuits are awesome! I love eating them plain, topped with homemade Raw sauerkraut, or alongside a serving of soup or salad.

> 1 cup dry raw buckwheat groats (see instructions, Appendix C)
>
> 1 cup sun-dried tomatoes
>
> 1 ½ cups raw pecans
>
> 1 ½ cups carrot pulp, gently packed*
>
> 2 cups zucchini, chopped
>
> ½ cup (reserved) sun-dried tomato soak water
>
> ½ cup fresh orange juice
>
> ⅓ cup nutritional yeast**
>
> ¼ cup tamari, wheat-free***
>
> 1 tablespoon onion powder
>
> 1 teaspoon garlic, pressed and packed

Soak and sprout your buckwheat groats per the instructions in Appendix C. *Once they are soaked and sprouted, you need 2 cups for this recipe, as they get larger from being soaked.*

Place the sun-dried tomatoes in a bowl and add enough water to cover them. Let them soak for up to an hour. Drain the water off into another bowl and keep ½ cup for use later in the recipe.

Use a food processor, fitted with the "S" blade, to process the pecans until coarsely ground. Add the remaining ingredients and process until pureed. Spread the mixture until it is about 1-inch high (this makes nice thick biscuits) onto a dehydrating tray fitted with a ParaFlexx non-stick sheet (these sheets are for Excalibur dehydrators. If you don't have one, you can use parchment paper).

Score into squares of desired size. Dehydrate at 135 degrees F for 75 minutes. Reduce the temperature to 105 degrees F and continue dehydrating another 10–12 hours. Flip the biscuits onto a dehydrator tray without ParaFlexx, and peel off the current ParaFlexx being used. Continue dehydrating until dry (approximately 18–24 hours, or longer if you want crunchier biscuits).

* Carrot pulp is what's left over after extracting juice from carrots. If you don't have a juicer to make the carrot juice, the following are some options:

- Is there a juicing (or health food) store that you could go to and order a carrot juice, then ask for the pulp in a separate cup? (Remember you need 1.5 cups gently packed.) As always, try to get organic.

- If you have a blender, you can blend some carrots with a little bit of water. Strain out the juice and the pulp will be left in the bag. You need a nut milk bag for this, or go to the hardware store and buy a paint strainer bag (they're cheaper.) Cheese cloth could work, but it'll likely get messy.

** This is not a Raw ingredient, but it adds a cheesy flavor to the biscuits as well as B-vitamins.

*** I usually use the reduced-sodium variety of wheat-free tamari, but it's delicious with either kind.

Cinnamon Banana Crispies

Yield 2 cups

This granola is simple and delicious. Heck, you can eat it like you would popcorn during the next movie you watch.

> 1 cup dry raw buckwheat groats (see instructions, Appendix C)
>
> ¼ cup water
>
> 2 bananas, peeled
>
> ¾ teaspoon cinnamon

Soak and sprout your buckwheat groats per the soaking instructions in Appendix C. Once the buckwheat groats are ready (they should be about 2 cups now that they're soaked and sprouted), place them in a bowl. Blend the water, bananas, and cinnamon. Pour the banana mixture over the buckwheat groats and stir to mix.

Pour about half of the mixture onto the center of a dehydrator tray fitted with a ParaFlexx sheet (you can use parchment paper if you don't have ParaFlexx sheets). Give the tray a little shimmy-shake to spread out the mixture a bit. Repeat these directions for the second half of the batter. Dehydrate at 135 degrees F for 60 minutes. Reduce the temperature to 105 degrees F and continue dehydrating another 5–7 hours. Flip the mixture onto dehydrator trays without ParaFlexx sheets and peel off the current ParaFlexx sheets being used. Continue dehydrating 4–8 hours, or until dry. Hold it over a bowl and crumble into the bowl.

Chocolate Banana Spiced Crispies

Yield 2 cups

For the chocolate princess (or prince) in you (or your kids!).

1 cup dry raw buckwheat groats (see instructions, Appendix C)

¼ cup water

2 bananas, peeled

3 tablespoons raw chocolate powder

¼ teaspoon cinnamon

Soak and sprout your buckwheat groats per the soaking instructions in Appendix C. Once the buckwheat groats are ready (they should be about 2 cups now that they're soaked and sprouted), place them in a bowl. Blend the water, bananas, chocolate, and cinnamon. Pour the banana mixture over the buckwheat groats and stir to mix.

Pour about half of the mixture onto the center of a dehydrator tray fitted with a ParaFlexx sheet (or you can try parchment paper if you don't have the ParaFlexx sheets). Give the tray a little shimmy-shake to spread out the mixture a bit. Repeat these directions for the second half of the batter. Dehydrate at 135 degrees F for 60 minutes. Reduce the temperature to 105 degrees F and continue dehydrating another 5–7 hours. Flip the mixture onto dehydrator trays without ParaFlexx sheets and peel off the current ParaFlexx sheets being used. Continue dehydrating 4–8 hours, or until dry. Hold it over a bowl and crumble into the bowl.

Quickie Garlic Chia Crisps

Yield 15–20 crisps (depending on how you break them apart)

½ cup chia seeds

¾ cup water

½ cup hemp seeds

2 cloves garlic

½ cup fresh basil leaves, packed

1 teaspoon fresh lemon juice

¼ teaspoon Himalayan crystal salt

¼ teaspoon onion powder

Set the chia seeds aside in a bowl. Blend the remaining ingredients until smooth. Pour the blended mixture over the chia seeds and stir until thoroughly mixed. Allow the mixture to sit for 10–15 minutes and stir again.

Transfer the mixture to a dehydrator tray lined with a ParaFlexx sheet and spread out the mixture. Dehydrate at 130–135 degrees F for one hour. Reduce the temperature to 105 degrees F and continue dehydrating for 8 hours. Flip the dehydrating mixture onto a dehydrator tray without a ParaFlexx sheet, and peel off the current ParaFlexx sheet being used. Continue dehydrating until dry (approximately 8–10 hours). Once they're done dehydrating, break into rustic looking crisps of different shapes and sizes.

Tropical Chia Pudding

Yield 3 cups

⅓ cup chia seeds

⅓ cup dried coconut, shredded and unsweetened

1 cup young Thai coconut water*

1 cup young Thai coconut meat, packed*

1 ½ cups mango, peeled, pitted, and chopped

4 dates, pitted and soaked 15 minutes

1 ½ teaspoons allspice

Place the chia seeds and dried coconut in a medium bowl and set aside. Blend the remaining ingredients until smooth and pour over the chia seeds and dried coconut. Stir together. Wait a few minutes as it starts to gel and stir again. Repeat this a few times. Enjoy immediately or refrigerate to enjoy later.

* You can purchase young Thai coconuts from health food stores or Asian markets. Unfortunately, they're rarely organic, and usually treated with chemicals to extend their shelf life during the trip from harvest to store. To learn how to crack open a young Thai coconut, visit my blog and check out my video here: KristensRaw .blogspot.com/2010/02/how-to-open-young-thai-coconut-video.html Alternatively, you can buy certified organic, Raw, unpasteurized, untreated coconut water and coconut meat. I have purchased this at Whole Foods (it's by *Body Ecology*), and you can find it in the freezer section.

Vibrant Green Chia Pudding

See photo at KristensRaw.com/photos.

Yield 3 cups

¼ cup + 2 tablespoons chia seeds

¼ cup + 2 tablespoons dried coconut, shredded and
   unsweetened

1 cup water

¼ cup hemp seeds

1 mango, peeled, pitted, and chopped

1 banana, peeled and chopped

1 cup spinach, packed

1 cup romaine lettuce, chopped and packed

1 tablespoon raw agave nectar

1 teaspoon vanilla extract

2 pinches nutmeg

1 pinch Himalayan crystal salt

Place the chia seeds and dried coconut in a medium bowl and set aside. Blend the remaining ingredients until smooth and pour over the chia seeds and dried coconut. Stir together. Wait a few minutes as it starts to gel and stir again. Repeat this a few times. Enjoy or refrigerate and enjoy later.

Power Superfruit Vanilla Spread

¾ cup raw cashews

⅓ cup goji berries

⅓ cup dried mulberries

¼ cup fresh orange juice

2 tablespoons goji berries soak water (a little more if needed)

1 teaspoon vanilla extract

2 pinches Himalayan crystal salt

Place the cashews in a bowl and cover with enough water by about an inch. Let them soak for 1 hour. Drain off the water and give them a quick rinse. Place the goji berries in a separate bowl and cover with water plus about an inch. Let them soak for 30–45 minutes. Reserve the goji berry soak water for use later in the recipe. Once the cashews and goji berries are ready, blend all of the ingredients together until smooth and creamy.

Serving Suggestions:

- Serve with sliced bananas, apples, pineapple, or any other fruit. Or, enjoy plain like a yogurt.

Cheezy Hemp Nacho Sauce

Yield approximately 1 ½ cups

This is one of my all-time BEST recipes. It has become famous making the Raw Fooder Internet rounds and the feedback is phenomenal. It's approved, coveted, devoured, and obsessed over by thousands of herbivores and omnivores alike!

⅓ **cup water**

1 **clove garlic**

2 **tablespoons fresh lemon juice**

1 **red bell pepper, seeded and chopped**

1 **cup hemp seeds**

2 ½ **tablespoons nutritional yeast flakes**

1 **tablespoon chili powder***

2 **teaspoons tamari, wheat-free**

½ **teaspoon Himalayan crystal salt**

½ **teaspoon garlic powder**

¼ **teaspoon cayenne pepper**

⅛ **teaspoon turmeric powder**

Blend all of the ingredients in a blender until creamy.

Serving suggestions:

- Dip veggies or corn chips (Raw or cooked) into this. This also makes a delicious dressing on a hearty salad with romaine lettuce, tomatoes, and cucumbers.

- For those eating cooked foods, this is an *awesome* sauce on top of veggie burgers!

* My favorite brand of chili powder is Simply Organic™.

Appendix A

· · · · · · · · · · ·

Raw Food Tips

MEASUREMENT CONVERSIONS

1 tablespoon = 3 teaspoons

1 ounce = 2 tablespoons

¼ cup = 4 tablespoons

⅓ cup = 5 ⅓ tablespoons

1 cup = 8 ounces

= 16 tablespoons

= ½ pint

½ quart = 1 pint

= 2 cups

1 gallon = 4 quarts

= 8 pints

= 16 cups

= 128 ounces

ORGANIC FOOD

According to the Organic Trade Association, "Organic agricultural production benefits the environment by using earth-friendly agricultural methods and practices. Here are some facts that show why organic farming is "the way to grow."

Choosing organically grown foods is one of the most important choices we can make. According to Environmental Working Group, "The growing consensus among scientists is that small doses of some pesticides and other chemicals can cause lasting damage to human health, especially during fetal development and early childhood."

I use organic produce and products for pretty much everything when it comes to my food. There are very few exceptions, and that would be if the recipe called for something I just can't get organic such as jicama, certain seasonings, or any random ingredient that my local health food store is not able to procure from an organic grower for whatever reason.

If you think organic foods are too expensive, then start in baby steps and buy a few things at a time. Realize that you're probably going to spend less money in the long run on health problems as your health improves, and going organic is one way to facilitate that.

The more people who choose organic, the lower the prices will be in the long run. Until then, if people complain about the prices of organic produce, all I can say is, "Your health is worth it!" Personally, I'm willing to spend more on it and sacrifice other things in my life if necessary. I don't need the coolest car on the block, I want the healthiest food going into my body! I like what Alice Waters says, "Why wouldn't you want to spend most of your money on food? Food is nourishment and good health. It is the most important thing in life, really."

Vote with your dollar! Here is something I do to help further this cause and you can, too. When I eat at a restaurant I always write on the bill, "I would eat here more often if you served organic food." Can you imagine what would happen if we all did this?

Bottom Line: It is essential to use organic ingredients for many reasons:

- The health benefits—superior nutrition, reduced intake of chemicals and heavy metals and decreased exposure to carcinogens. Organic food has been shown to have up to 300% more nutrition than conventionally grown, non-organic produce. And, a very important note for pregnant women: pesticides can cross the placenta and get to the growing life inside of you. Make organics an extra priority if you're pregnant.
- To have the very best tasting food ever! I've had people tell me in my raw food demonstration classes that they never knew vegetables tasted so good—and one of the main reasons is because I only use organic.
- Greater variety of heirloom fruits and vegetables is the result of growing organic produce.
- Cleaner rivers and waterways for our earth and its inhabitants, along with minimized topsoil erosion. Overall, organic farming builds up the soil better, reduces carbon dioxide from the air, and has many environmental benefits.

GOING ORGANIC ON A BUDGET

Going organic on a budget is not impossible. Here are things to keep in mind that will help you afford it:

- Buy in bulk. Ask the store you frequent if they'll give you a deal for buying certain foods by the case. (Just make sure it's a case of something that you can go through in a timely fashion so it doesn't go to waste). Consider this for bananas or greens especially if you drink lots of smoothies or green juice, like I do.

- See if local neighbors, family or friends will share the price of getting cases of certain foods. When you do this, you can go beyond your local grocery store and contact great places (which deliver nationally) such as Boxed Greens (BoxedGreens.com) or Diamond Organics (DiamondOrganics.com). Maybe they'll extend a discount if your order goes above a certain amount or if you get certain foods by the case. It never hurts to ask.

- Pay attention to organic foods that are not very expensive to buy relative to the conventional prices (bananas, for example). Load up on those.

- Be smart when picking what you buy as organic. Some conventionally grown foods have higher levels of pesticides than others. For those, go organic. Then, for foods that are not sprayed as much, you can go conventional. Avocados, for example, aren't sprayed too heavily so you could buy those as conventional. Here is a resource that keeps an updated list: foodnews.org/walletguide.php

- Buy produce that is on sale. Pay attention to which organic foods are on sale for the week and plan your menu around that. Every little bit adds up!

- Grow your own sprouts. Load up on these for salads, soups, and smoothies. Very inexpensive. Buy the organic seeds in the bulk bins at your health food store or buy online and grow them yourself. Fun!

- Buy organic seeds/nuts in bulk online and freeze. Nuts and seeds typically get less expensive when you order in bulk from somewhere like Sun Organic (SunOrganic.com). Take advantage of this and freeze them (they'll last the year!). Do the same with dried fruits/dates/etc. And remember, when you make a recipe that calls for expensive nuts, you can often easily replace them with a less expensive seed such as sunflower or pumpkin seeds.

- Buy seasonally. For instance, don't buy a bunch of organic berries out of season (eat more apples and bananas in the fall and winter). Also, consider buying frozen organic fruits, especially when they're on sale!

- Be content with minimal variety. Organic spinach banana smoothies are inexpensive. You can change it up for fun by adding cinnamon one day, nutmeg another, vanilla extract yet another. Another inexpensive meal or snack is a spinach apple smoothie. Throw in a date or some raisins for extra pizzazz. It helps the budget when you make salads, smoothies, and soups with ingredients that tend to be less expensive such as carrots (year round), bananas (year round), zucchini and cucumbers (in the summer), etc.

KRISTEN SUZANNE'S TIP: A NOTE ABOUT HERBS

Hands down, fresh herbs taste the best and have the highest nutritional value. While I recommend fresh herbs whenever possible, you can substitute dried herbs if necessary. But do so in a ratio of:

3 parts fresh to 1 part dried

Dried herbs impart a more concentrated flavor, which is why you need less of them. For instance, if your recipe calls for three tablespoons of fresh basil, you'll be fine if you use one tablespoon of dried basil instead.

THE INFAMOUS SALT QUESTION: WHAT KIND DO I USE?

All life on earth began in the oceans, so it's no surprise that organisms' cellular fluids chemically resemble sea water. Saltwater in the ocean is "salty" due to many, many minerals, not just sodium chloride. We need these minerals, not coincidentally, in roughly the same proportion that they exist in... guess where?... the ocean! (You've just gotta love Mother Nature.)

So, when preparing food, I always use sea salt, which can be found at any health food store. Better still is sea salt that was deposited into salt beds before the industrial revolution started spewing toxins into the world's waterways. My personal preference is Himalayan Crystal Salt, fine granules. It's mined high in the mountains from ancient sea-beds, has a beautiful pink color, and imparts more than 84 essential minerals into your diet. You can use either the Himalayan crystal variety or Celtic Sea Salt, but I would highly recommend sticking to at least one of these two. You can buy Himalayan crystal salt through KristensRaw.com/store.

KRISTEN SUZANNE'S TIP: START SMALL WITH STRONG FLAVORS

Flavors and Their Strength

There are certain flavors and ingredients that are particularly strong, such as garlic, ginger, onion, and salt. It's important to observe patience here, as these are flavors that can be loved or considered offensive, depending on who is eating the food. I know people who want the maximum amount of salt called for in a recipe and I know some who are highly sensitive to it.

Therefore, to make the best possible Raw experience for you, I recommend starting on the "small end" especially with ingredients like garlic, ginger, strong savory herbs and seasonings, onions (any variety), citrus, and even salt. If I've given you a range in a recipe, for instance ¼–½ teaspoon Himalayan crystal salt then I recommend starting with the smaller amount, and then tasting it. If you don't love it, then add a little more of that ingredient and taste it again.

Start small. It's worth the extra 60 seconds it might take you to do this. You might end up using less, saving it for the next recipe you make and voila, you're saving a little money.

LESSON #1: It's very hard to correct any flavors of excess, so start small and build.

LESSON #2: Write it down. When an ingredient offers a "range" for itself, write down the amount you liked best. If you use an "optional" ingredient, make a note about that as well.

One more thing to know about some strong flavors like the ones mentioned above... with Raw food, these flavors can intensify the finished product as each day passes. For example, the garlic in your soup, on the day you made it, might be perfect. On day two, it's still really great but a little stronger in flavor. And by day three, you might want to carry around your toothbrush or a little chewing gum!

Here's a Tip to Help Control This

If you're making a recipe in advance, such as a dressing or soup that you won't be eating until the following day or even the day after that, then hold off on adding some of the strong seasonings until the day you eat it (think garlic and ginger). Or, if you're going to make the dressing or soup in advance, use less of the strong seasoning, knowing that it might intensify on its own by the time you eat it. This isn't a huge deal because it doesn't change that dramatically, but I mention it so you won't be surprised, especially when serving a favorite dish to others.

KRISTEN SUZANNE'S TIP: RIPENESS AND STORAGE FOR YOUR FRESH PRODUCE

- I never use green bell peppers because they are not "ripe." This is why so many people have a hard time digesting them (often belching after eating them). To truly experience the greatest health, it's important to eat fruits and vegetables at their peak ripeness. Therefore, make sure you only use red, orange, or yellow bell peppers. Store these in your refrigerator.

- A truly ripe banana has some brown freckles or spots on the peel. This is when you're supposed to eat a banana. Store these on your countertop away from other produce, because bananas give off a gas as they ripen, which will affect the ripening process of your other produce. And, if you have a lot of bananas, split them up. This will help prevent all of your bananas from ripening at once.

- Keep avocados on the counter until they reach ripeness (when their skin is usually brown in color and if you gently squeeze it, it "gives" just a little). At this point, you can put them in the refrigerator where they'll last up to a week longer. If you keep ripe avocados on the counter, they'll only last another couple of days.

- Avocados, like bananas, give off a gas as they ripen, which will affect the ripening process of your other produce. Let them ripen away from your other produce. And, if you have a lot of avocados, separate them. This will help prevent all of your avocados from ripening at once.

- Tomatoes are best stored on your counter. Don't put them in the refrigerator or they'll get a "mealy" texture.

- Pineapple is ripe for eating when you can gently pull a leaf out of the top of it. Therefore, test your pineapple for ripeness at the store to ensure you're buying the sweetest one possible. Just pull one of the leaves out from the top. After 3 to 4 attempts on different leaves, if you can't gently take one of them out, then move on to another pineapple.

- Stone fruits (fruits with pits, such as peaches, plums, and nectarines), bananas and avocados all continue to ripen after being picked.

I have produce ripening all over my house. Sounds silly maybe, but I don't want it crowded on my kitchen countertop. I move it around and turn it over daily.

For a more complete list of produce ripening tips, check out my raw food lifestyle book, *Kristen's Raw: The EASY Way to Get Started & Succeed with Raw Food* (available at Amazon.com).

YIELDS AND SERVING AMOUNTS

Each recipe in this book shows an approximate amount that the recipe yields (the quantity it makes). I find that "one serving" to me might be considered two servings to someone else, or vice versa. Therefore, I tried to use an "average" when listing the serving amount. Don't let that stop you from eating a two-serving dish in one sitting, if it seems like the right amount for you. It simply depends on how hungry you are.

WHAT IS THE DIFFERENCE BETWEEN CHOPPED, DICED, AND MINCED?

Chop

This gives relatively uniform cuts, but doesn't need to be perfectly neat or even. You'll often be asked to chop something before putting it into a blender or food processor, which is why it doesn't have to be uniform size since it'll be getting blended or pureed.

Dice

This produces a nice cube shape, and can be different sizes, depending on which you prefer. This is great for vegetables.

Mince

This produces an even, very fine cut, typically used for fresh herbs, onions, garlic and ginger.

Julienne

This is a fancy term for long, rectangular cuts.

WHAT EQUIPMENT DO I NEED FOR MY NEW RAW FOOD KITCHEN?

I go into much more detail regarding the perfect setup for your Raw vegan kitchen in my book, *Kristen's Raw: The Easy Way to Get Started & Succeed at the Raw Food Vegan Diet & Lifestyle*, which is a must read for anybody who wants to learn the easy ways to succeed with living the Raw vegan lifestyle. For the purposes of having the goal to live a lifestyle that is increasingly

Raw, here are the main pieces of equipment you'll want to get you going:

- An excellent chef's knife (6–8 inches in length—non-serrated). Of everything you do with Raw food, you'll be chopping and cutting the most, so invest in a great knife. This truly makes doing all the chopping really fun!
- Blender
- Food Processor (get a 7 or 10-cup or more)
- Juicer
- Spiralizer or Turning Slicer
- Dehydrator—Excalibur® is the best company by far and is available at KristensRaw.com. Also, see coupon at the back of this book.)
- Salad spinner
- Other knives (paring, serrated)

For links to online retailers that sell my favorite kitchen tools and foods, visit KristensRaw.com/store.

SWEETENERS

The following is a list of sweeteners that you might see used in my recipes. It's important to know that the healthiest sweeteners are fresh whole fruits, including fresh dates. That said, dates sometimes compromise texture in recipes. As a chef, I look for great texture, and as a health food advocate, I lean towards fresh dates. But as a consultant helping people embrace a Raw vegan lifestyle, I'm also supportive of helping them transition, which sometimes means using Raw agave nectar, or some other easy-to-use sweetener that might not have the healthiest ranking in the Raw food world, but is still much healthier than most sweeteners used in the Standard American Diet.

Most of my recipes can use pitted dates in place of Raw agave nectar. There is some debate among Raw food enthusiasts as to whether agave nectar is Raw. The companies I use (Ultimate Superfoods and Madhava®) claim to be Raw and say they do not heat their Raw agave nectar above 118 degrees F. If however, you still want to eat the healthiest of sweeteners, then bypass the Raw agave nectar and use pitted dates. In most recipes, you can simply substitute 1–2 pitted dates for 1 tablespoon of Raw agave nectar. Dates won't give you a super creamy texture, but the texture can be improved by making a "date paste" (pureeing pitted and soaked dates—with their soak water, plus some additional water, if necessary—in a food processor fitted with the "S" blade). This, of course, takes a little extra time.

If using Raw agave nectar is easier and faster for you, then go ahead and use it; just be sure to buy the Raw version that says they don't heat the agave above 118 degrees F (see KristensRaw.com/store for links to this product). And, again, if you're looking to go as far as you can on the spectrum of health, then I recommend using pitted dates. Most of my recipes say Raw agave nectar because that is most convenient for people.

Raw Agave Nectar

There are a variety of agave nectars on the market, but again, not all of them are Raw. Make sure it is labeled "Raw" on the bottle as well as claiming that it isn't processed above 118 degrees F. Just because the label says "Raw" does not necessarily mean it is so... double check and make sure it also claims not to be heated above the 118 degrees F cut-off. Agave nectar is noteworthy for having a low glycemic index. For links to some of my favorite brands, visit:

KristensRaw.com/store

Dates

Dates are probably the healthiest of sweeteners, because they're a fresh whole food (I'm a big fan of Medjool dates). Fresh organic dates are filled with nutrition, including calcium and magnesium. I like to call dates "Nature's Candy."

Feel free to use dates instead of Raw agave nectar or honey in Raw vegan recipes. If a recipe calls for ½ cup of Raw agave, then you can substitute with approximately ½ cup of pitted dates (or more).

You can also make a recipe of Date Paste to replace Raw agave (or to use in combination with it). It's not always as sweet as agave, so you might want to adjust the amount according to your taste by using a bit more Date Paste.

Date Paste

It's great to keep this on hand in the refrigerator so you have it available and ready to use. Date Paste is easy to make and should take you less than 10 minutes to prepare once your dates are soaked. Store it in an airtight container in the refrigerator (a glass mason jar is perfect).

> **15 Medjool dates, pitted, soaked 15 minutes (reserve soak water)**
>
> **¼–½ cup reserved "soak water"**

Using a food processor, fitted with the "S" blade, puree the ingredients until you have a smooth paste.

Honey

Most honey is technically raw, but it is not vegan by most definitions of "vegan" because it is produced by animals, who therefore are at risk of being mistreated. While honey does not have the health risks associated with animal by-products such as eggs or dairy, it can spike the body's natural sugar levels. Agave nectar has a lower, healthier glycemic index and can replace any recipe you find that calls for honey, in a 1 to 1 ratio.

Maple Syrup

Maple syrup is made from boiled sap of the maple tree. It is not considered Raw, but some people still use it as a sweetener in certain dishes.

Rapadura®

This is a dried sugarcane juice, and it's not Raw. It is, however, an unrefined and unbleached organic whole-cane sugar. It imparts a nice deep sweetness to your recipes, even if you only use a little. This is a nice alternative to the icky, processed white sugar out there, which might be of interest to someone who is transitioning to healthier eating.

Stevia

This is from the leaf of the stevia plant. It has a sweet taste and doesn't elevate blood sugar levels. It's very sweet, so you'll want to use much less stevia than you would any other sweetener. My mom actually grows her own stevia. It's a great addition in fresh smoothies, for example, to add some sweetness without the calories. When possible, the best way to have stevia is to grow it yourself.

Yacon Syrup

This sweetener is reported to have a low glycemic index, making it very attractive to people. It has a molasses-type flavor that is very enjoyable. You can replace Raw agave nectar with this sweetener, but keep in mind that Raw agave nectar is sweeter. The brand I usually buy is Navitas Naturals, which is available at NavitasNaturals.com.

The Right Chocolate — Raw Chocolate

I love the fact that one of my greatest pleasures in life is actually good for me. My favorite way to have chocolate is in the "Raw" form — straight from the cacao bean — because Raw chocolate is unrefined, unprocessed, all natural and filled with nutrients.

The health benefits of Raw chocolate are significant, with a resume that includes loads of antioxidants (and I really mean loads! loads! loads!) as well as plenty of magnesium, fiber, iron, calcium, zinc, copper, vitamins A, B1, B2, B3, C, E, and more. One of the main attractions to pure chocolate is that of the heart health benefits. The flavonoids (organic compounds) found in cacao can help prevent clogged arteries and lower blood pressure.

So, yes, Raw chocolate is indeed great and offers us a number of health benefits. However, that does not mean that we should go overboard when eating it. A little bit goes a long way and moderation, as always, is important with this superfood.

EATING WITH YOUR EYES

Most of us, if not all, naturally eat with our eyes before taking a bite of food. So, do yourself a favor and make your eating experience the best ever with the help of a simple, gorgeous presentation. Think of it this way, with real estate, it's always location,

location, location, right? Well, with food, it's always presentation, presentation, presentation.

Luckily, Raw food does this on its own with all of its naturally vibrant and bright colors. But I take it even one step farther—I use my best dishes when I eat. I use my beautiful wine glasses for my smoothies and juices. I use my fancy goblets for many of my desserts. Why? Because I'm worth it. And, so are you! Don't save your good china just for company. Believe me, you'll notice the difference. Eating well is an attitude, and when you take care of yourself, your body will respond in kind.

Recommended Reading & Viewing

For a complete and detailed list of my favorite kitchen tools, products, and various foods (all available online), please visit:

KristensRaw.com/store.

BOOK & DVD RECOMMENDATIONS

I highly recommend reading the following life-changing books:

- *Diet for a New America*, by John Robbins
- *The Food Revolution*, by John Robbins
- *The China Study*, by T. Colin Campbell
- *Skinny Bitch*, by Rory Freedman
- *Food Matters* DVD
- *Food, Inc.* DVD
- *Earthlings* DVD
- *The Future of Food* DVD

Appendix B

· · · · · · · · · ·

Resources

The resources listed in this appendix are mostly raw, but you will also see a few items that are not raw.

BANANAS (FROZEN)

To make frozen bananas, simply peel (ripe) bananas, place them in a baggie or container, and put them in the freezer. I like to use my FoodSaver®, because it keeps the bananas from getting ice crystals on them. Having frozen bananas in your freezer at all times is a smart move. They are fantastic in smoothies, and they make a deliciously fun raw ice cream (just throw them in the food processor and puree them into a soft serve, raw vegan ice cream).

BREAD (SPROUTED)

You can buy this at the health food store. A couple of my favorite brands are *Good for Life* and *Manna Organics*.

CACAO LIQUOR (RAW)

This is the result of whole cacao beans that have been peeled and cold-pressed, which forms a paste. I use this to make a number of raw chocolate recipes. It comes in a block form and I melt it into a thick liquid using my dehydrator (or you can use a double boiler). It's bitter so I add sweetener. This is available from NavitasNaturals.com

CACAO NIBS (RAW)

These are partially ground cacao beans. They can be used in a variety of ways from toppings to raw vegan ice cream or yogurt. They add texture to shakes and smoothies, and you can make raw chocolates with them. They are available from NavitasNaturals .com and other sources online.

CAROB (RAW)

A lot of the carob you find in the store is toasted. I like to use raw carob, which has a wonderful flavor (caramel-like) and can be used in many recipes such as smoothies, nut milks, desserts, and more. There is a link for raw carob at KristensRaw.com/store.

CHIA SEEDS

These are called the "Dieter's Dream Food." Chia seeds are praised for many things including their fantastic nutrient profile, which proudly boasts iron, boron, essential fatty acids, fiber, and more. Add to that the claims that they may improve heart health, reduce blood pressure, stabilize blood sugar, help people lose weight from giving them extra stamina, energy, and curbing hunger, and you might become a fan of these little guys, too. They're superstars in my book. You can find a link for them at KristensRaw.com/store.

CHOCOLATE (CACAO) POWDER (RAW)

This is formed after the whole cacao beans have been peeled and cold-pressed. Then, the cacao oil is extracted and a powder remains. I use this in many recipes from making raw chocolate desserts to smoothies to soups to dressings and more. This is available from NavitasNaturals.com and other sources online.

COCONUT AMINOS

This is a seasoning sauce that can be used in place of tamari and namo shoyu. Available from the company, Coconut Secret, it's raw, enzymatically alive, organic, gluten-free, and soy-free. For more details, check out CoconutSecret.com. It's also available at some Whole Foods Markets.

COCONUT BUTTER OR *COCONUT SPREAD*

Coconut butter is not to be confused with plain coconut oil. Coconut butter is actually the coconut oil and coconut meat together in one jar. This can be eaten by the spoonful and it can also be used in desserts, smoothies, spreads, and more. There are two companies that I buy this from: WildernessFamilyNaturals.com offers a product they call "Coconut Spread" while Artisana calls theirs coconut butter. You can find the Artisana Coconut Butter at many health food stores including Whole Foods Market.

To make coconut butter easier (i.e., softer) to use, consider warming it in a dehydrator (at a low temperature).

DIAYA™ CHEESE

This is an amazing vegan cheese (not raw) that is taking the vegan world by storm. If you know of someone who misses artery-clogging, animal based cheese, then turn them on to this. It's soy-free, dairy-free, gluten-free, corn-free, and preservative-free. You can read more details at DaiyaFoods.com. I buy it from Whole Foods Market.

GOLDENBERRIES

These are also known as Incan Berries or Cape Gooseberries. They are basically a little dried fruit similar in shape to a raisin, and golden in color. The first time I tried these, I immediately thought, *"Move over crappy sour patch kids, it's time for something way more delish and oh-so-healthy at the same time!"* Goldenberries will throw a party in your mouth. These are available at NavitasNaturals .com

GOJI BERRIES

These little ruby colored jewels (also known as wolfberries) are a mega popular superfood because of their amazing nutrient content. They have 18 amino acids, including the 8 essential amino acids. Plus, their antioxidants are through the roof! The taste is a cross between a dried cherry and dried cranberry. I enjoy them plain and used in various recipes. My favorite source for them is Navitas Naturals (they're also available at various health food stores), and there is a link for them at KristensRaw.com/store.

GREEN POWDER(S)

Green powders are chock-full of powerful raw and alkalizing nutrition. My favorites are *Health Force Nutritionals' Vitamineral Green* and *Amazing Grass' Wheat Grass Powder*. Health Force Nutritionals also makes a green powder for pets called *Green Mush*. You will find links to these products at KristensRaw.com/store.

HEMP FOODS

Hemp is commonly referred to as a "superfood" because of its amazing nutritional value. Its amino acid profile dominates with the 8 essential amino acids (10 if you're elderly or a baby), making it a vegetarian source of "complete" protein. Manitoba Harvest is my favorite source for hemp products. I use their hemp seeds, hemp butter, hemp protein powder and hemp oil to make many delicious raw vegan recipes.

HERBAMERE™

This is an alternative to plain salt. It is a blend of sea salt and 14 organic herbs. It's a nice change of pace from plain salt. This is available on Amazon.com, other websites, and in some health food stores.

LUCUMA POWDER

Lucuma is a fun ingredient that is popular with Raw fooders. NavitasNaturals.com offers lucuma as a whole food powder, which adds a lovely sweetness to recipes with a flavor that has been described as a cross between sweet potato and maple. I love using lucuma powder in various raw recipes for smoothies, ice cream, cheesecake, nut milk, cookies, brownies, and more. There are other online sources for lucuma powder as well.

MACA POWDER

Maca is a plant that is used as a root and medicinal herb. Many people claim it gives them tons of energy and increased stamina for exercise, long workdays, and even libido! Personally, I'm not a huge fan of maca's flavor (to me, it smells like feet and tastes accordingly—haha), but this is one of the most popular superfoods among Raw vegans (so many people love it!), and for good reason with its reputed benefits. (Did I mention libido?) There is a link for maca powder at KristensRaw.com/store.

MESQUITE POWDER

This comes in a powder form that offers nutrition with a smoky, malt-like, and caramel flavor. This is available from NavitasNaturals .com and other online sources.

MISO

My all-time favorite source of organic miso is South River Miso. It's the ONLY brand I use. They have so many amazing flavors (including soy-free varieties). Check them out at SouthRiver-Miso.com. Two of my favorite flavors are *Dandelion Leek* and *Garlic Red Pepper*. You can use other brands of light or dark miso in place of the fancier flavors I've used in these recipes, but South River Miso is amazing so I highly recommend it.

MULBERRIES

These are lightly sweet with a wonderful texture that makes it hard to stop eating them. I consider these delights a superfood because of their nutrient content, including a decent source of protein. They are available from NavitasNaturals.com.

NON-DAIRY (PLANT-BASED) MILK

There are plenty of plant-based milks available for purchase in various grocery stores. They are not raw, but they are vegan and many are available as organic, which I highly recommend. Here are some options: almond, hemp, rice, soy, hazelnut, oat, and coconut. Plus, there are different flavors within those varieties such as plain, vanilla, and chocolate.

NUT / SEED BUTTERS (RAW)

Raw nut butters can be bought at most health food stores or you can easily make your own (simply grind nuts with a dash of Himalayan crystal salt in a food processor, fitted with the "S" blade, until you get a nut or seed butter. You might choose to add a little olive oil to help facilitate the processing. This could take 3–8 minutes).

There are different varieties available such as hemp seed butter, almond butter, hazelnut butter, pecan butter, sunflower seed butter, pumpkin seed butter, cashew butter, walnut butter, macadamia nut butter, and more. Some excellent brands are *Living Tree Community, Rejuvenative Brands, Wilderness Poets (online)*, and *Artisana*. I usually buy them from Whole Foods Market.

OLIVES (RAW)

I truly love *Essential Living Foods'* Black Bojita Olives. They are juicy, fresh, and delicious. It's hard to stop at eating only one! They are available at Whole Foods Market and online at EssentialLivingFoods.com. I also use *Living Tree Community's* Sun-Dried Olives in some recipes. They're different in taste and texture than the Black Bojita Olives.

OLIVE OIL (RAW)

I enjoy two truly raw olive oils: *Living Tree Community* (LivingTreeCommunity.com, also available at some Whole Foods Markets) and *Wilderness Family Naturals* (available online at WildernessFamilyNaturals.com).

ORANGE PEEL POWDER

This is a powder, which is the dried, finely ground orange peel (it's where you'll find many of the orange's nutrients, too). This is available from MountainRoseHerbs.com (They also have lemon peel powder.)

PROTEIN POWDER

I use various raw vegan protein powders to get extra protein in my life. My favorites are hemp and sprouted raw brown rice protein powders.

In general, when I'm drinking the sprouted raw brown rice protein powder (by just mixing it with water), I like the chocolate and natural flavors from *Sun Warrior* or the plain flavor of *Sprout Living's EPIC Protein.* Hemp foods, *Sun Warrior* protein powder and *Sprout Living* protein powder are available at KristensRaw.com/store.

RAPADURA

This is a dried sugarcane juice, and it is not Raw. It is, however, an unrefined and unbleached organic whole-cane sugar. I buy mine at Whole Foods Market.

RIGHTEOUSLY RAW CACAO BARS (EARTH SOURCE ORGANICS)

Even though this is not an ingredient in which you'd use to make a recipe, I had to mention it here (it's an actual product for organic, raw, vegan chocolate bars). In my opinion, this is the best raw chocolate bar on the market. My favorite flavor is the Caramel Cacao but they also sell Goji, Maca, and Acai. Sometimes I just don't have time to make my own raw chocolate and sometimes I'm just plain lazy. In both cases, I run to Whole Foods Market for these (you can also buy them online direct from the company: earthsourceorganics.com). If your Whole Foods doesn't stock these... tell them to do it! Check out my blog post where I talked about my first encounter with these divine treats.

> http://kristensraw.blogspot.com/2010/review-earth-source-organics.html

ROLLED OATS

I use traditional organic oats from SunOrganic.com or raw oats available at NaturalZing.com.

SAUERKRAUT (RAW, UNPASTEURIZED)

You can buy sauerkraut from the health food store or make it yourself (my favorite way). If you choose to buy it from the store, be sure to get a brand that is organic, raw, and unpasteurized. Two brands that I like are *Gold Mine Natural Foods* and *Rejuvenative Foods* (they're both great, but my overall preference is Gold Mine Natural Foods).

However, making your own is the best. It's incredibly easy and fun. For directions on making your own sauerkraut, please see my blog posts and video here:

> http://kristensraw.blogspot.com/2009/07/how-to-make-sauerkraut-video-raw.html

SESAME OIL (RAW)

You can get this from RejuvenativeFoods.com.

STEVIA

Stevia is an all-natural sweetener from the stevia plant. It has a sweet taste and doesn't elevate blood sugar levels. It is very sweet, so you will want to use much less stevia than you would any other sweetener. I buy mine from Navitas Naturals (available at NavitasNaturals.com)

SUN-DRIED OLIVES

I buy the brand *Living Tree Community* at Whole Foods Market or online at LivingTreeCommunity.com.

SUNFLOWER LECITHIN

This is popular for its choline content, and it's also used as an emulsifier in recipes. Soy lecithin is a common "go-to" source for this purpose, but not everyone wants a soy product. That is all changed now that sunflower lecithin is available. I like adding it to raw soups, smoothies, desserts, and more. You can find a link for it at KristensRaw.com/store.

TEECCINO®

This is an alkaline herbal "coffee" (it's not really coffee) that my family loves since giving up regular coffee. It is available at many health food stores like Whole Foods Market. It's also available online (Amazon.com). For details about the awesomeness of this product, check out Teeccino.com.

VEGGIE BURGER

I LOVE Organic *Sunshine Burgers* veggie burgers, which I buy in the freezer department of Whole Foods Market. Check out their website at SunshineBurger.com.

WAKAME FLAKES

The wakame flakes that I use are from Navitas Naturals. Here is what they have to say about this particular product on their website at NavitasNaturals.com:

"One of the most hearty vegetables of the sea, wakame is in fact an algae that is amongst the oldest living species on Earth. This sea green has been used extensively in traditional Japanese, Chinese, and Korean cuisine as an important health food and key component of Eastern medicine for centuries. Wakame is a balanced combination of essential organic minerals including iron, calcium, and magnesium, alongside valuable trace minerals as well. Additionally, wakame is well known for its detoxifying antioxidants, Omega 3 fatty acids (in the form of Eicospentaenoic acid), and body-building vegetable proteins. Wakame also provides many vitamins like vitamin C and much of the B spectrum, and serves as an excellent source of both soluble and insoluble fiber."

Impressive, huh?

WHEAT GRASS POWDER

I use Amazing Grass' Wheat Grass Powder available at KristensRaw.com/store.

YACON SYRUP, POWDER, AND SLICES

This is an alternative sweetener offering a low glycemic index so it's commonly viewed as diabetic friendly. According to Navitas-Naturals.com (the brand I prefer for yacon products), *"... yacon tastes sweet, the sugar of inulin is not digestible and simply passes through the body. Therefore, yacon only contains about half the calories of an average sugar source. Secondly, FOS (promotes the production of healthy probiotics within the body, which can contribute to better digestion and colon health."*

Appendix C
....
Soaking & Dehydrating

SOAKING AND DEHYDRATING NUTS AND SEEDS

This is an important topic and might be brand new to you, but it's really easy (and cool, if I do say so myself). When using nuts and seeds in Raw vegan foods, you'll find that recipes sometimes call for them to be "soaked" or "soaked and dehydrated." Here is the low-down on the importance and the difference between the two.

Why Should You Soak Your Nuts and Seeds?

Most nuts and seeds come packed by Mother Nature with enzyme inhibitors, rendering them harder to digest. These inhibitors essentially shut down the nuts' and seeds' metabolic activity, rendering them dormant—for as long as they need to be—until they detect a moisture-rich environment that's suitable for germination (such as rain). By soaking your nuts and seeds, you trick the nuts into "waking up," shutting off the inhibitors so that the enzymes can become active. This greatly enhances the nuts' digestibility for you and is highly recommended if you want to experience Raw vegan food in the healthiest way possible.

Even though you'll want to soak the nuts to activate their enzymes, before using them, you'll need to re-dry them and grind them down anywhere from coarse to fine (into a powder almost like flour), depending on the recipe. To dry them, you'll need a dehydrator. (If you don't own a dehydrator yet, then, if a recipe calls for "soaked and dehydrated," just skip the soaking part; you can use the nuts or seeds in the dry form that you bought them).

Drying your nuts (but not yet grinding them) is a great thing to do before storing them in the freezer or refrigerator. They will last a long time and you'll always have them on hand, ready to use.

In my recipes, I use nuts and seeds that are "soaked and de-hydrated" (that is, dry) unless otherwise stated in the directions as needing to be "soaked" (that is, wet).

Some nuts and seeds don't follow the enzyme inhibitor rule and therefore don't need to be soaked. These are:

- Macadamia nuts
- Brazil nuts
- Pine nuts
- Hemp seeds
- Most cashews

An additional note... there are times when the recipe will call for soaking, even though it's for a type of nut or seed without en-zyme inhibitors, such as Brazil nuts. The logic behind this is to help soften the nuts so they blend into a smoother texture, es-pecially if you don't have a high-powered blender. This is helpful when making nut milks, soups and sauces.

A Note About Flax and Chia Seeds

Flax and chia seeds don't need to be soaked if your recipe calls for grinding them into a powder. Some recipes will call to soak the seeds in their "whole-seed" form, before making crackers and bread, because they create a very gelatinous and binding texture when soaked. You can soak flax or chia seeds in a ratio of one-part seeds to two-parts water, and they can be soaked for as short as 1 hour and as long as up to 12 hours. At this point, they are ready to use (don't drain them). Personally, when I use flax seeds, I usually grind them and don't soak them. It's hard for your body to digest "whole" flax seeds, even if they are soaked. It's much easier for your body to assimilate the nutrients when they're ground to a flax meal.

INSTRUCTIONS FOR SOAKING NUTS AND SEEDS

When a recipe in this book calls for "1 cup of seeds" (or nuts), for instance, do the following:

- Place 1 cup of the dry product in a bowl.
- Fill the bowl with enough water to cover the seeds or nuts by about one inch.
- Let the bowl sit on your countertop for the designated time instructed in the recipe.
- When the time is up, drain the water and rinse the seeds or nuts. (Discard the soak water. Do not use it for anything, as it usually contains enzyme inhibitors.)

The seeds or nuts are now ready to use in the recipe. If you can't make the recipe immediately, you can keep the nuts/seeds in a covered container in the refrigerator for up to three days. To prevent them from drying out, you might consider giving them a daily rinse and drain.

When the recipe requires soaking, here are the average times for various nuts and seeds:

- Cashews, brazil nuts, pine nuts, and macadamia nuts (1–2 hours)
- Sunflower seeds and pumpkin seeds (6–8 hours)
- Walnuts and pecans (6–8 hours)
- Almonds (10–12 hours)

Dehydrating Nuts

After soaking, draining, and rinsing your nuts, spread them out on a mesh dehydrator sheet and dehydrate them at 130–140 degrees F for about an hour. Then, reduce the temperature to 105–115 degrees F, and continue dehydrating them until they're completely dry, which can take up to 24 hours.

INSTRUCTIONS FOR SOAKING & SPROUTING BUCKWEAT GROATS

Buckwheat groats double in volume after they've been soaked (before dehydrating). For example, if a recipe calls for 2 cups of buckwheat groats (soaked), then it means that you originally start with about 1 cup of dry buckwheat groats.

The following are basic instructions for soaking and sprouting buckwheat groats. The amount shown in this example is for 1 cup of dry raw buckwheat groats, which will yield about 2 cups soaked and sprouted (be sure to check the specific recipe you are making and use the amount called for in it):

- Take 1 cup of dry buckwheat groats and put them in a bowl.

- Fill the bowl with enough water to cover the buckwheat by about one inch. Allow them to sit on your countertop for 8–12 hours.

- After they have soaked, drain off the water, rinse well, and transfer the buckwheat groats to a colander that you have set over a bowl (to catch the dripping water).

- Gently cover the bowl with a paper towel, and let the buckwheat sprout for 24–36 hours, rinsing/draining the buckwheat about every 12 hours.

If you have leftover soaked-and-sprouted buckwheat after you take the amount needed for the recipe (or perhaps you just made extra), simply put any leftovers on a dehydrator tray and dehydrate until dry. You can eat them plain, in trail mix, as a raw cereal, stirred into vegan yogurt, or top your next salad with them. They're delightful!

INSTRUCTIONS FOR SOAKING DRIED FRUITS

Some recipes call for reconstituted fruits that are often available as dried fruit, such as goji berries, goldenberries, prunes, raisins, and others.

To reconstitute your dried fruits, place them in a bowl on your countertop, and cover them with water by about a ½ inch. Let them soak for 30–60 minutes or until soft.

In many cases, you can discard the soaking water when you are done... or drink it! BUT WAIT! Some recipes require you to save the soak water for use later in the recipe.

SUN-DRIED TOMATOES

By far, the best sun-dried tomatoes are those you make yourself with a dehydrator. If you don't have a dehydrator, make sure you buy the "dry" sun-dried tomatoes, usually found in the bulk section of your health food market. Don't buy the sun-dried tomatoes that are packed in a jar of oil.

Also… don't buy sun-dried tomatoes if they're really dark (almost black) because these just don't taste as good. Again, I recommend making them yourself if you truly want the freshest flavor possible. It's really fun to do!

Making your own sun-dried tomatoes is super easy. Plus, it saves money! Simply slice your organic tomatoes and dehydrate them in your dehydrator until dry. The thinner you slice them, the faster they will dry. My favorite brand of dehydrator is the Excalibur, available at:

KristensRaw.com/store

(See coupon at the back of this book.)

Instructions for Soaking Sun-Dried Tomatoes

To soak your sun-dried tomatoes, place them in a bowl on your countertop and cover them with water by about a ½–¾ inch. Soak them for 30–60 minutes or until soft—the time will vary, depending on the thickness of the slices.

As with soaking dried fruits, in many cases, you can discard the soaking water when you're done… or drink it! BUT WAIT! Some recipes require you to reserve the soak water for use later in the recipe.

I make my own "sun-dried" tomatoes, using thin slices of tomato and my Excalibur dehydrator. Because I make mine thin, I can break them with my hands, which is what I do before soaking them in some recipes. If you use store-bought sun-dried tomatoes, they are probably thicker and harder to break (or cut) before soaking. Therefore, I recommend soaking them first, and then chopping them after they're done soaking, if needed.

PROPER DEHYDRATION TECHNIQUES

Dehydrating your Raw food at a low temperature is a technique that warms and dries your food while preserving its nutritional integrity. You are removing moisture from the food so bacteria, yeast and mold can't grow and spoil the food. The food becomes lighter in weight because the water weight is gone. Having a dehydrator can be a lot of fun, especially for people transitioning to a Raw vegan lifestyle.

Dehydrating some of your Raw food is a great aspect to the Raw vegan lifestyle, because it adds variety, as well as shelf life. With a dehydrator, you can have crunchy foods, warm foods, marinated foods with a texture reminiscent of cooked food, and foods that can last a long time in your pantry, refrigerator or freezer.

One of the biggest challenges people think they'll encounter with Raw food cuisine is not having enough time to prepare the food and/or not having enough variety. Bringing a dehydrator into your life solves both of these issues.

When you use a dehydrator you can also save a lot of money. I find myself easily saving money when I make my own dehydrated foods as opposed to buying pre-dried, packaged foods.

When using a dehydrator, it is recommended that you begin the dehydrating process at a temperature of 130–140 degrees F for about an hour. Then, lower the temperature to 105 degrees F for the remaining time of dehydration. Using a high temperature such as 140 degrees F, in the initial stages of dehydration, does not destroy the nutritional value of the food. During this initial phase, the food does the most "sweating" (releasing moisture), which cools the food. Therefore, while the temperature of the air circulating around the food is about 140 degrees F, the food itself is much cooler. These directions apply when using an Excalibur Dehydrator because of their Horizontal-Airflow Drying System.

I recommend Excalibur dehydrators because of their first-class products and customer service. For details, visit the Raw Kitchen Essential Tools section of my website at KristensRaw.com/store. Additionally, I have a great recipe book, or ebook if desired, dedicated to dehydrating Raw vegan foods. There are plenty of delicious recipes as well as tips and tricks for using a dehydrator in this book. *Kristen Suzanne's Easy Raw Vegan Dehydrating* is available for purchase at Amazon.com and on my website:

KristensRaw.com/raw_recipe_books.php

As a reader of this book, you are entitled to a 10% discount off Excalibur dehydrators and products: